GOLDEN ISLANDS

AN Ⓘ INVOLVEMENT MEDIA BOOK

GOLDEN ISLANDS
OF THE CARIBBEAN

FRED WARD

With photographs by
FRED WARD & TED SPIEGEL

CROWN PUBLISHERS, INC. • NEW YORK

Cover: the British Virgin Islands.

*Title page: beach on Dutch
St. Maarten.*

*Half-title page: Emerald Pool,
Dominica*

Library of Congress Catalog
Card Number: 72-84302
ISBN: 0-517-50166X
Produced for the publisher
by Involvement Media, Inc.,
from a concept and design
by Ted Spiegel
Printed in the Netherlands
by Smeets Offset, Weert

Published in the United States, its possessions and Canada by Crown Publishers, Inc.,
419 Park Avenue South, New York, N.Y. 10016.

Published simultaneously in the United Kingdom by Thomas Nelson & Sons, Ltd., London.

PHOTO CREDITS

FRED WARD — Black Star: 1, 21-23, 26-32, 49-52, 54, 56-59, 60 (top), 61-62, 64, 81-87, 92-95, 124-128, 142-145, 150 (top), 154-156

TED SPIEGEL — Black Star: cover, 2-3, 24-25, 50-53, 55, 88-91, 96, 113-123. RICHARD MEEK: 141, 146-149, 153. ROLF BRUDERER for BWIA: 150 (bottom), 151; for AIR FRANCE: 60 (bottom), 63. JOHN LAUNOIS — Black Star: 152

HISTORICAL ILLUSTRATIONS

WEST INDIA COMMITTEE — London: 8, 47 (right), 69, 75 (4), 79, 99, 101, 103, 104, 107, 111, 131, 133, 135, 138 (3). UNIVERSITY OF FLORIDA LIBRARY: 34, 39, 41, 44, 45. NEW YORK PUBLIC LIBRARY: 12, 67 (right), 72, 73. LIBRARY OF CONGRESS: 9, 10, 17. UNIVERSITY OF MIAMI LIBRARY: 36, 37, 47 (left). ENGLISH HARBOUR MUSEUM, ANTIGUA: 43

Contents

I.
THE VIRGIN ISLANDS

Explorers, conquerors, gold, the Spanish Main, privateers, buccaneers, pirates, sugar, slaves, exploitation, revolt, abolition, sun, beaches, tourism—from this incredible mélange the dramatic history of the West Indies whirls like a hurricane through a tropical sea. No archipelago on earth has so many political divisions, such a complex past, or so large an impact on the world's most powerful nations as this chain of islands in the Caribbean Sea.

In 1492 Christopher Columbus discovered only a section of the West Indies—the Bahamas, Cuba, and Hispaniola. He was so sure he had found the Orient that he named the islands "The Indies" and the docile Arawak inhabiting them "Indians." Although Columbus failed to find a new route to the East, the voyage brought him fame and success and the privilege of making the first traveler's report from a new world. Enthusiastically he wrote the treasurer of Aragon: "The Caribbean Islands are as beautiful as any in the world, and no area is luckier in its climate." He referred to the Lesser Antilles as the Arawak did, calling them "Caribbees" after the warlike Carib Indians that controlled them.

After centuries more of exploration, charts of the Caribbean now show 5,000 islands, rocks, cays, reefs, and sandbars. Fewer than two hundred are inhabited or played a significant role in the region's stormy past. Renaissance cartographers called all the islands the "Antilles" after the mythical continent "Antilla" which was thought to exist somewhere in the Atlantic. Later the large islands of Cuba, Hispaniola (now shared by Haiti and the Dominican Republic), Jamaica, and Puerto Rico became the "Greater Antilles." All the rest—the Virgin Islands, the Leewards, the Windwards, Barbados, Trinidad, and Tobago—were called the "Lesser Antilles," the subjects of this book.

The Leewards and the Windwards, two central groups comprising over 30 islands, define a gentle arc eastward toward the Atlantic. To seamen, "windward" means the direction from which the wind is blowing and "leeward" means the direction toward which it is going. The smaller islands on the northern Caribbean lie leeward of Barbados, the important British landfall; therefore, Guadeloupe through Anguilla were called the "Leewards." Since the prevailing trade winds blow from the east, islands windward of the Spanish-held South American mainland, Grenada through Dominica, became known as the "Windwards."

The majority of the Caribbean islands are really mountain-tops thrust boldly through the water when the turbulent sea covered an area that was even more geologically active than it is today. During the Miocene Period about thirty-five million years ago, a massive earth movement called the Alpine shaped the islands to their present dimensions. That intensive volcanic activity accompanied this period of disturbance is evidenced to this day on Guadeloupe, St. Vincent, and Martinique. Relatively flat Barbados, Anegada, Anguilla, Barbuda, and parts of Guadeloupe, Antigua, and St. Martin were born of coral. Periodic dynamic shifts in the earth's crust raised the remains of trillions of tiny hard-shelled organisms deposited over the millennia on the ocean floor.

During the second trip to the New World, Columbus's luck faltered on the morning of November 14, 1493. When the Admiral's fleet of seventeen galleons approached the northern coast of Santa Cruz (later changed by the French to St. Croix), he sent a small excursion party onto the beach at Salt River. Just as the group was returning, they came upon a canoe filled with crimson-painted natives led by a woman. After a moment's startled disbelief the Spaniards, who tried to cut the natives off from shore, met with a volley of arrows dipped in deadly manchineel sap. Though severely wounded and outflanked, the Indians continued to fight fiercely from the water after their canoe was rammed. Finally, all of them were either killed or captured for display before the Spanish king. As a result of this Carib hostility, Columbus did not land on any other Virgin Island. It is thought that as he looked back at the misty peaks, the scene reminded him of the tale of St. Ursula and her 11,000 virgins who died resisting a horde of barbarian rapists.

Columbus had now encountered two Caribbean tribes—the Arawak and the Caribs. In 1493 the Virgin Islands were the dividing line between them. The Arawak, an older tribe to the region, occupied the Greater Antilles and the Bahamas. The menacing Caribs had actually consumed the Arawak in the Lesser Antilles. It is likely that much of Spain's fervor would have been diminished if Columbus had clashed with the Caribs on his first voyage.

Exploration rivalry arose immediately between Spain and Portugal, since, as a result of African coastal forays, Portugal claimed certain exclusive rights for herself. Both countries appealed to the Vatican for a solution. In 1493 Alexander VI issued four Papal Bulls that divided the world for discovery. Spain relished her new prizes—all the New World except what is now eastern Brazil.

As Columbus completed his third and fourth voyages, the lack of a sea passage thwarted Spain's dream of finding an ocean route to the treasures of the East. By the middle of the sixteenth century,

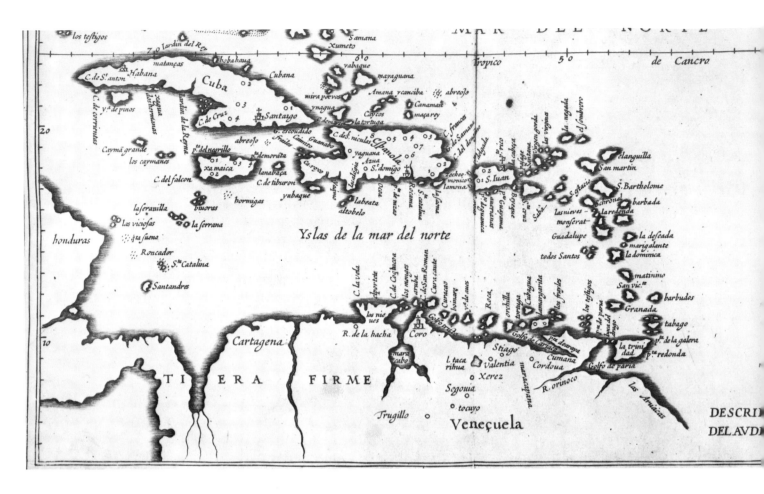

the Spaniards had killed the Indians or transported them from the northern Caribbean, thus making the Virgins "safe" for European occupancy. Since agricultural colonies were never her goal, Spain saw no use for the islands. The Spanish were obsessed with gold. Columbus once wrote the King and Queen of Spain, ". . . all . . . nations that possess pearls, precious stones, and other articles of value, take them to the ends of the earth to exchange them for gold. Gold is the most precious of all commodities, and he who possesses it has all he needs in this world, as also the means of rescuing souls from purgatory, and restoring them to the enjoyment of paradise." Fabulous stories of great wealth later came from Cortés, Balboa, and Pizarro in Mexico, Central America, and Peru. So Spain's monarchs decided to leave the remainder of the Lesser Antilles to the Caribs and develop the larger settled islands as bastions to protect the treasure caravans that plied their way from Central America to Cadiz.

The Virgin Islands held far greater appeal for the French and the English, who were not at all satisfied with the Pope's dispensation of the New World. Since Spain was convinced that she ruled the area by divine right, conflicts were inevitable and not long in coming. The first intrusion into Spain's exclusive preserve came from the celebrated privateer John Hawkins. Born into a seafaring

N DEL DISTRICTO
A DELA ESPAÑOLA
3

Christopher Columbus rightfully deserves full credit for opening the New World to European exploration and exploitation. During his incredible four voyages to the West Indies, he discovered, charted, and named most of the Caribbean islands. In this 1590 map of the area, the islands still bear the names given by Columbus, the Admiral of the Ocean Seas—and the symbolic flag of Spain, as ordained in the Papal Bull of 1493.

family at Plymouth, England, he was well aware that the Spanish settlers in the Caribbean had begun to import slaves for labor and that a "Triangle of Trade" concept was developing. Operating from a home port in Europe, a ship would make a run to Guinea on Africa's western coast to take on slaves, cross the Atlantic (the "Middle Passage") to sell them in the West Indies, and return home with agricultural products, gold, and silver from the Caribbees.

In 1562 Hawkins successfully broke the Portuguese slave trading monopoly by stopping on the African coast to take on a load of recently captured blacks. During two voyages he sold slaves in the Spanish colonies (illegally, according to Spain's laws) and captured three of their treasure ships. During this period slavery was not unknown in Europe. Prisoners of war were often kept in bondage as laborers. Still, there was no precedent for actively seeking out humans for the express purpose of turning them into slaves. The development of the practice took a significant turn at the beginning of Hawkins's "troublesome" third voyage. In October, 1567, he took six ships from Plymouth and headed for Guinea, where he found only a few natives being held for shipment. The king of Sierra Leone was in the process of attacking a town of 8,000 natives. By bargaining his aid in the king's siege in return for some of the captured blacks, Hawkins fostered one of the most dismal aspects

of dealing in people, the deliberate waging of intertribal wars for the purpose of obtaining prisoners to sell. After a series of mishaps and a disastrous fight with the Spanish at San Juan de Ulúa on Mexico's Caribbean coast, Hawkins limped back to England with one ship carrying just 15 of the original 400 sailors. Nevertheless, the expedition was considered a success because the sale of 600 slaves had brought a profit in gold and pearls. More important than this single voyage was the new relationship among European nations. The fate of the West Indies was set—what Spain could not protect, England and France were determined to possess.

Hawkins had not concerned himself with the Virgin Islands, since they had no trading colonies. Their great worth was realized when his cousin, the notorious Francis Drake, began his incredible exploits among the emerald peaks. Also born in Plymouth, Drake spent his boyhood aboard a boat. His affinity for the sea was to contrast greatly with his island adversaries, the Spanish soldiers who only became sailors in the service of their king.

Drake was the first of a new breed of adventurer, the freebooter, from the Dutch *vrijbuiter* meaning "free booty." Content to let someone else find the loot, he would then attempt to steal it. In July, 1572, Drake began attacking the Spanish Main with speed and elusiveness, leaving his victims so puzzled and stunned that they were powerless to find him. During this lawless period, more than 200 Spanish frigates operated in the West Indies, some of which he seized several times. The slippery sea dog never stayed long in one place and was never captured. Strangely, his audacity was matched by gentleness, for he never destroyed a ship unless during heated battle nor killed any men taken prisoner. It would be difficult to find a similar record in West Indian history.

El Draqui, as the Spanish called him, viewed the Caribbean as his own lake and found that the practically deserted Virgin Islands were perfect for his line of work. He discovered a deep water passage through the Virgins that still bears his name, Sir Francis Drake Channel. High atop a St. Thomas hill a bench for tourists commemorates the spot where Drake supposedly sat. From here he could watch the fleet leaving Puerto Rico on its mission of protecting the richly laden treasure ships.

Throughout all this activity Spain continued to regard the Caribbean as her property. By the 1580s the English-Spanish conflict had been building for about 30 years, and a decisive battle seemed inevitable and even desirable. King Philip II put his wealth and his best efforts into floating an awesome fleet, the Spanish Armada. England rallied her most seaworthy warships under the now-famous cousins, Hawkins and Drake. The two forces clashed in the English Channel in 1588. Although outnumbered, the British fleet fought desperately for a week and gained control. Only 60 of the original 100 Spanish ships survived the battle. In her defeat Spain started a slow spiral of impotence which greatly diminished her influence in the Caribbean. Anxious for development, other European countries rapidly filled the void, and after years of Spanish neglect, the Virgin Islands moved into the mainstream.

St. Croix was the first of the now U.S. Virgin Islands to be fought over by the world powers. French, English, and Dutch settlers all arrived about 1625. They feuded among themselves, and were overrun briefly by the Spanish from Puerto Rico. Finally, the French returned with determination and gained control.

Denmark made its first entry into the islands by occupying St. Thomas in 1666. It was only a moderately profitable venture for the Danes until an enterprising young governor opened the area as a slave-trade center. Because of the demand for labor and the inability of the colonists to do business with their traditional European adversaries, the capital city of Charlotte Amalie immediately became the biggest and richest slave market in the world. In another adroit move, Denmark opened the harbor to all, pirates and privateers included, and established a duty-free port in return for free passage of its ships at sea. Charlotte Amalie acquired a scarlet reputation as the wildest city in the Caribbean.

No period in history was more lawless than the age of piracy, nor any place more favorable than the West Indies for this nefarious lifestyle. Foreign powers fought continual battles; relatively unprotected ships convoyed treasure; merchant vessels plied their trade alone; and enforcement bodies were almost nonexistent. The topography was ideal, with numerous coves and hideaways, and most of the islands had water, wood, and food. Since all Spain's colonies were legally required to trade exclusively with Spanish ships, the settlers were commodity-poor. Captured goods found ready buyers in Cuba and other Spanish islands.

Pirates also used the Virgin Islands as a convenient place to live and debauch. Charlotte Amalie's clientele included Blackbeard, Bluebeard, and Captain Kidd. Few questions were asked of anyone, but a local planter did note the unwritten understanding: "A privateer can use the harbor as long as he likes, but a pirate may not lie there more than 24 hours." He went on to explain that both groups would capture a ship and cargo and rob its crew but that "a pirate then kills the crew while a privateer spares their lives." There were enough exceptions on both sides to disprove this generalization. In either event, no moral distinctions were made in Charlotte Amalie when the illicit booty was accepted for sale.

The planter's practical definition aside, pirates were outlaws, whereas privateers operated with a "letter of marque" from their

After being displaced twice by the Spanish, a new band of rogues took to the sea to harass and plunder West Indian shipping. The buccaneers knew no allegiance and honored no code except their own. Spanish treasure fleets were a special target for the marauding sailors.

government. They were legally empowered to engage in trade, and could be called on in time of war to participate as part of the government's navy—a flamboyant cross between the national guard and the merchant marine. But, in the West Indies the designations became hazy as captains and ships moved easily between lawful and illegal activity; what was considered legitimate by England was branded robbery by Spain.

In piracy, as in other professions, certain practitioners surged to the top. None was more repulsive, or successful, or feared than Edward Teach (or Thatch), better known as Blackbeard the Pirate. Born in Bristol, England, he learned his trade early as an apprentice on a pirate's boat in the West Indies. Soon, student surpassed master, and Teach struck out on his own.

Teach studied the psychology of piracy and determined that surprise and terror were tantamount to overpowering the victim. A burly man, he designed his own appearance to make any reasonable sailor beg for mercy from the onset. His dirty, thickly matted black beard swung against his waist. Readying for battle, he braided this hanging mass of hair, blood, and food into pigtails which he tied with brightly colored ribbons. Twining the braids through his bushy hair, Teach topped his weird coiffure with a floppy black hat and stuck two long slow-burning sulfur matches out the sides by his ears. Black knee boots, a chest festooned with pistol sashes, and a motley assortment of weapons under his belt turned Ned Teach into Blackbeard the Pirate, a dangerous, fearsome, and filthy adversary.

Teach's enormous hands wielded a ten-pound cutlass. As he leapt onto the deck of a doomed ship, he started slashing in wild arcs that did not stop until the crew yelled "quarter" or lay dead in the gore. Many a merchant captain, upon encountering this glowering apparition aboard his ship, was sure he was being attacked by the devil himself—exactly the effect Blackbeard wanted.

St. Thomas prospered during the piracy era. So many ships brought such fabulous wealth to the island that huge warehouses were needed, and rows of terra-cotta buildings went up along the harbor at the then unheard-of cost of $50,000 each. Soaring arches over great, thick masonry walls kept the goods cool, and inlaid floors of Italian tiles and Spanish marble satisfied the luxurious taste of the new business tycoons.

Piracy waned as island governments gained stability and offered greater protection to their ports and ships. Blackbeard's death in 1718 tolled a knell for the rambunctious epoch. Profits soon came from less glamorous agriculture. After Denmark's success in St. Thomas, she sent a small group across the narrow channel to colonize St. John in 1717. They imported slaves, laid out estates, and built great houses. The island was deforested, and sugar was planted on every hill. Flourishing with the prosperous activity, a genteel planter society began to evolve. Some peace was even established with the English in the British Virgin Islands, who had thwarted earlier Danish attempts to claim St. John.

By 1733 a network of handmade roads connected the manor houses, fields, and mills of 106 plantations. The owners lived fairly comfortable lives on breeze-swept hills above the coast, but during the harvest periods the slaves toiled from dawn to dusk to feed the groaning bulletwood rollers of the sugar windmills. When a series of crop failures made the planters reluctant to spend scarce cash even to buy food for the slaves, consistently high tensions between the two races reached a critical stage.

On November 23, some of the slaves detailed to take firewood into the small Danish fort at Coral Bay concealed weapons in their bundles and quickly overcame the surprised soldiers. Within a few hours about 25 planter families had been hacked to death near the fort. At Caneel Bay, on the other end of the island, estate owners hurriedly sent their women and children by boat to the safety of St. Thomas. After six months the rebels were finally conquered, but then only with the help of French troops from Martinique. (All the islands feared an uprising, particularly, as in St. John, where planters were outnumbered ten to one.) Although there is some confusion regarding the death of the last band of slaves, the most plausible report has them leaping to their death on the rocks below Mary's Point.

Despite the problems caused by the slave revolt, sugarcane was still profitable and the Danes were ready to expand. In 1733 one of their companies was prosperous enough to buy St. Croix from the French crown for $1,500,000. Within 12 years 375 plantations spread across its 85 square miles. Cane was king until 1848, when the Danish crown, in keeping with the world's growing humanism, abolished slavery in the islands. Without pirates' trade and profits from slave-raised sugarcane, the Virgins drifted into a long sleep.

President Lincoln wanted to accept Denmark's offer to sell her islands, but the U.S. Senate refused to vote the necessary $5,000,000. As World War I neared in 1914, the United States needed a naval base for monitoring sea approaches to the Panama Canal Zone. For a new price of $25,000,000, on March 31, 1917, the U.S. bought St. Thomas, St. John, St. Croix, and a few miscellaneous rocks and cays. But the anticipated boom was so slow in coming that land in St. Croix was still selling for $10 an acre in 1940 and only $400 in 1950.

All three islands are matured versions of their past. The rollicking heritage of St. Thomas continues with its reputation as the "swinging" Virgin Island. Varied night life, superb beaches, and considerably more social activity than on the other U.S. Virgins attracts the younger set of tourists. With charter sailing, cruise ships, and a jet airport, St. Thomas is still the crossroads of the

Caribbean. More than a million tourists spend well over $100,-000,000 a year reveling in the ultimate of "free ports." Enticements are lower list prices and the favorable ruling that U.S. citizens may return through customs with double the usual amount of foreign purchases before paying taxes.

The beautiful and durable warehouses of the eighteenth century now form the basis of the main shopping street in Charlotte Amalie. They still contain a store of wealth, not contraband but opulent beyond a pirate's dream. Enhanced by modern decor and lighting, the old stone walls arch over a new flood of "duty-free" shoppers, looking for bargains in the smart boutiques. Elaborate displays offering 500 varieties of perfumes, 50 brands of cameras and optical devices, or 100,000 bottles of liquor compete for the visitor's purse. One of the conditions of sale by the Danes was that the islands would remain free ports, and so the same trading incentive that attracted the pirates of old continues to draw shoppers from all over the world looking for a "steal" of a buy.

St. John, only three miles to the east of St. Thomas, is the quiet island. Enough planters remained after the slave revolt to reestablish sugar prosperity only to see it lost again with abolition in 1848. Soon after, the last plantation ceased operation, the freed Africans began to garden and fish, and the island drifted into ano-

The great natural harbor at Charlotte Amalie, centrally located in the northern Caribbean, contributed to St. Thomas's impressive rise as a commercial center. Denmark welcomed ships from every country, turning the entire island into a free port. Warehouses filled as merchants and pirates amassed enough of the world's treasures to turn the port into the "Emporium of the West Indies."

nymity. Even purchase by the United States in 1917 had only nominal influence on obscure St. John.

When Laurance Rockefeller arrived in the 1950s, he found the island still basically unspoiled, somewhat as Columbus had seen it. Buying all the available property, about three-quarters of the island, with its adjacent ocean bottom, Rockefeller donated it as parkland for the people of the United States. In the Virgin Islands National Park, paved roads and gravel trails meander through the old sugar plantations over tracks once plied by sugar carts making their way to the busy mills. Here and there, vestiges of crumbling stone estates still survive the encroaching "bush," and copper boiling pots lie askew at a ruin's edge. As nature slowly and deliberately obliterates the interloping sugar fields, the great roofless buildings testify that something important once happened here.

St. John is not all history. There is great appeal in forest-covered hills and solitary trails. It is also still possible to explore a private little white sand beach all alone. If company is desired, there are two places to enjoy it. Caneel Bay Plantation, Rockefeller's very popular and luxurious resort on the western coast, is a hotel designed to blend into the natural surroundings. More basic is the beachside National Park campground on Cinnamon Bay, commonly booked for tent reservations a year in advance.

St. Croix is the epitome of a plantation isle, still largely given over to agriculture with its "plantocracy" surviving in old families living on ancient estates. Although three times larger than St. Thomas, St. Croix attracts only a tenth the number of cruise ships and a fifth of the overnight guests, but many people have been discovering the island for home sites. By the late 1950s, St. John had become a park and St. Thomas a shopping center; but St. Croix was still languishing as a sugar-dependent backwater. In 1958 the United States government supplied assistance in the form of a tax concession. Any product whose value was increased by more than 100 percent due to work done in the territories could be exported to the States tax free. With more job opportunities St. Croix freed herself from the millstone of a one-crop economy.

Industry responded immediately, creating a huge industrial complex on the southern coast. Two sprawling installations, an oil refinery and an aluminum plant, now dominate the landscape. A promising new concept in business utilizes local labor to do assembly work for 16 watch companies. It has proved economical to buy parts and subassemblies from Swiss, Japanese, Hong Kong, and German suppliers and ship them to St. Croix, where women in "clean rooms" meticulously fit the tiny pieces together. About four million watch movements are then exported each year to the United States.

St. Croix's two towns, Frederiksted to the west and Christiansted to the east, are living reminders of West Indian villages

three centuries ago. Stone and brick sidewalks passing beneath arched pillars lead from modern shops to brightly painted gingerbread houses. Even Fort Christiansvaern is quaint, more like a stage set than a serious defensive position. The Danish heart of Christiansted has been declared a National Historic Site.

The captains of a fleet of small single-masted sailing boats wait each morning in Christiansted's old harbor for the vacation sailors to pack their lunches and climb aboard. Light-hearted impromptu racing enlivens the five-mile run to Buck Island Reef National Monument. A white sand beach on the uninhabited island provides an idyllic picnic area, complete with Park Service facilities and enhanced by an ocean panorama of St. Croix. Around the eastern point gentle swells blur the surface that conceals the object of all this attention—Buck Island's reef. Conveying St. Croix's storybook theme underwater, a submerged marked trail guides the snorkeler where fantastic corals become fairy castles and hundreds of tiny crystalline fish perform in a dreamworld aquarium.

The British Virgin Islands are unusual in the West Indies in that no country ever seriously challenged England's control over them. Popular with the buccaneers, and the pirates who came after, these 40-odd islands and rocks offered coves for hiding and secluded beaches for repairs and maintenance. In the days before

The most tragic part of the horrible saga of West Indian slavery was the "Middle Passage," or month-long sea voyage from Africa. Terrified blacks, brutally torn from their homeland, were packed into stifling holds and carried off to Caribbean bondage. Though plantation owners logically guarded their investment, the blacks were treated as little more than farm animals.

drydocks, wooden-hulled boats in tropical waters had to be periodically careened—that is, beached and pulled over on their sides. Barnacles were scraped off and the planks were treated against boring sea worms. Vulnerable at these times, the men used the many indentations along Virgin Island coasts to provide security.

Although the terms *buccaneer* and *pirate* are often used interchangeably, the men had separate origins and divergent careers. The buccaneers were the jetsam of the seas. Homeless, without ties to family or country, their ranks were largely filled with refugees from Spain's 1629 raid on St. Kitts. Mutineers, shipwrecked sailors, destitute farmers, and escaped prisoners joined their numbers, and they all migrated to Hispaniola which basically had been abandoned by the Spanish. There the motley crew found abundant land and plenty to eat. Deriving their name from their cuisine, the squatters came to be called "buccaneers" after the French *boucanier*, which means "one who cures his meat over a *boucan*," or open fire. The buccaneers might have led a peaceful life had not Spain made a last desperate attempt to exercise control over the region. In 1638 Spaniards overpowered and removed the French from Tortuga, and also tried to eliminate the onlooking buccaneers. Having been twice wronged, the survivors vowed it would not happen again. Forthwith, they formed the society of the "Brethren of the Coast" and took to sea. For 30 years anything Spanish was considered fair game and plunder was their primary aim.

Even their initial encounter was a roaring success. In the dead of night 28 compatriots clambered aboard a galleon with pistols and cutlasses flashing. After overcoming several hundred startled Spaniards, the buccaneers set the crew free and sailed the treasure ship to France, where they retired and lived on their investments. Such achievement was irresistible to other Brethren. The gratifying combination of revenge and profit potential caused the Spanish much misery in the following decades.

In the beginning the buccaneers were principally English. They kept their loyalties pure by never attacking a British ship, concentrating instead on those of Spain, Portugal, and France. Understandably pleased that others were harassing the Spanish at no expense to her, England opened the pleasures of Port Royal to the buccaneers. Other favorite lairs were Tortuga and the Caymans. No matter how ruthless they were under sail, the Brethren were perfect citizens in the towns, where they were welcomed. It was good business and common sense, rather than high morals, that held them on the straight and narrow; for they needed ports in which to sell their plunder, to play, and to reprovision. Their own "shore patrols" made sure that no maiden was molested and all bills were paid promptly. Violators of the code were shot and chained up on the dock to rot in public, as powerful, albeit reeking, examples to the rest.

Few traces remain of this legendary prologue. Once the lusty days of the reckless sea rovers faded, the British islands tended to go unnoticed by history. Only recently have they begun to emerge from their obscurity. In 1966 Queen Elizabeth II became the first English monarch to see the British Virgin Islands, even though Great Britain has had some claim on them for over three hundred years. With a promising future, they are still not large or prosperous enough to become independent.

Tortola, the capital, is the biggest island and has most of the British Virgin Island inhabitants. Only a few seasons ago the main streets of Road Town reverberated with the grunts and squeals of roaming pigs. Dawn was heralded by the resounding cacophony of determined roosters, and the near-vertical hills above echoed to the vibrating calls of grazing sheep and goats. Today, it is quite different. The town is coming alive, and morning sounds are made by building machinery. Homes radiate onto the grassy hills and a new wharf and shopping area rise on landfill where the harbor used to be. A modern hotel occupies old Fort Burt, and condominiums are rising along the shore. The population tide is reversing as new residents seek out the "undiscovered Caribbean." Of the 10,000 people who live in the British Virgins, over 2,000 call Road Town home.

Just south of Tortola, on a small isle called Dead Chest, the dreaded Blackbeard supposedly abandoned a mutinous crew. This act inspired Robert Louis Stevenson to write, in *Treasure Island*, "Fifteen men on a dead man's chest, Yo-ho-ho, and a bottle of rum." Modern castaways welcome being marooned on the white sand beaches. Around each spit of land beckons still another palm-rimmed crescent. So clear is the water that boats seem suspended transparently above a West Indian Xanadu of variegated coral studded with brilliantly colored tropical fish.

Horse Shoe Reef, the graveyard of over three hundred vessels, lies almost completely hidden just south of Anegada. Once a constant hazard to sailors, the barely submerged obstacle ripped open ships reaching for deep water, strewing their cargoes along the ocean floor. Now, even a shallow dive over a wreck will reveal cannons and various coral-encrusted remains. Fortune hunters continue to poke around the ruins hoping to find a chest of gold. The real treasures are jeweled fishes, each inlaid with iridescent brilliants, unmatched by the kings' ransom lost here. With expert free-dives to over a hundred feet, local fishermen hand-catch lobsters, while giant groupers and jewfish patrol the lip of the reef. Sharks, the wolves of the sea, seem always lurking in the shadows.

The Baths on Virgin Gorda are among the strangest geological formations in the Antilles. Huge granite boulders, some three stories high, appear stockpiled at water's edge, awaiting an idle Hercules to skim them over a glass-calm sea. Inside deep caverns, secret channels flow into a labyrinth of shallow pools. Mysterious echoes play upon the walls, and eerie highlights bathe swimmers in a gray-green luster. Farther north, another Rockefeller resort, Little Dix Bay, secludes thatched cottages around a tranquil bay to create a harmonious setting for relaxation. Sea-island cotton, instead of sugar, was Virgin Gorda's money crop. The white-puffed plants are used as ornamentals on the hotel grounds and some still grow on the low hills which were once cultivated all the way down to the beaches. On the windswept eastern shore an old Spanish copper mine yields small amounts of blue-green ore.

West Indian diversity is apparent even in an area as small as the Virgin Islands. The differences to be noted with each new port are among the greatest charms of Caribbean island-hopping. For instance, only three miles away from vibrant St. Thomas rests St. John, where no raucous activity interrupts the peaceful tone. Although close enough so that one is clearly visible from the other, the sister islands seem to be separated by time rather than distance. A blend of their temperaments is discernible in St. Croix, as the influence of Danish plantation life gradually recedes with new construction and the introduction of modern industry.

So close they are practically intertwined, the British Virgin Islands and their U.S. neighbors have distinct personalities. Accents and attitudes immediately communicate the change in countries, but, in spite of these noticeable differences, it is altogether remarkable that the two groups of islands, tied to governments thousands of miles away, cooperate so fully. The British subjects work in dynamic St. Thomas and return home with U.S. dollars to spend as their own currency. Despite different inflections, all Virgin Islanders speak English. However, it is their harmonious spirit, not money or words, that proves islands can live together in peace.

Structured of coral, the reef is a natural wonderland, a cool blue world sheltering creatures of intricate, iridescent design. Buck Island Reef National Monument off St. Croix displays a treasure trove of ocean sculptures. Snorkelers glide through staghorn coral over a self-guided underwater trail; glass-bottomed boats provide a long view for the less intrepid.

Christiansted's Danish heart is protected as a National Historic Site, but modernization is conspicuous elsewhere on St. Croix. Watch-assembly, aluminum, and oil compete with tourism as income producers.

In the marketplace where his ancestors once stood on a slave dealer's auction block, this St. Thomas boy proudly offers a delicate flowering plant. Nearby, eighteenth-century warehouses have been converted into chic boutiques. Shelves laden with English china, French crystal, and Scandinavian silver tempt dollars out of tourists' pockets. Bound by the purchase treaty of 1917 to maintain the free port status established during Danish colonial days, the U.S. has fashioned an economic boom in Charlotte Amalie. Crowds of bargain-hunting sun-seekers buy silks, jewels, and cognacs to fill their airline carry-on bags. Citizens returning from U.S. possessions of Guam and the Virgin Islands enjoy customs exemptions for $200 in goods and one gallon of liquor. From everywhere else it's $100 and one quart.

Unruffled by the flurry of activity on the other U.S. Virgins, St. John lazes tranquilly in the sun. Ghostly remains such as the ruins at Annaberg are a mute testament to the days of sugar glory, when 90 percent of the island rippled in cane fields. Sparrow hawks nest among the stones that once housed thousands of slaves toiling to produce rum, sugar, and molasses. The 1733 uprising brought death to most of the Africans, devastation to the industry, and an end to the island's importance. Much of the land was recently purchased by Laurance Rockefeller and donated to the United States as the Virgin Islands National Park. Trunk Bay, with its offshore underwater trail, is the most popular of the Park's powdery white sand beaches.

Overleaf
Once a pirates' haven, the British Virgin Islands now welcome seclusion-minded vacationers.

No more bizarre sight exists in the Caribbean than the Baths on Virgin Gorda. At the southern end of the island an enormous jumble of huge granite boulders is heaped at water's edge, as if abandoned by giants after a monumental game of tossup. Forming asymmetrical rooms with vaulted cathedral arches, the stones surround shimmering pools that ebb and flow with the tides. Sea echoes abound, and with the filtered sunshine refracting through the foam, a natural sound and light show is created. Nearby, the sparkling Caribbean accents a sun-dappled vacationer at Little Dix Bay, a gracious beach resort that brought development to the long forgotten island. A desalination plant provides drinking water for the growing community. Clear seas and a multitude of undulating peaks make the Virgin Islands among the best sailing and vacationing areas in the world.

II.
THE DUTCH & FRENCH ANTILLES

Exotic ports in moonlit nights, cruise ships gliding toward towering peaks—these romantic dreams become reality for many visitors to the Caribbees owned by France and Holland. Other European mother countries have tried various legal arrangements to maintain ties. Some British West Indian islands are still colonies; most are independent and only loosely associated with England. The French Antilles are legally and culturally integral parts of France. Dutch islanders enjoy the status and rights of their European countrymen.

St. Martin (St. Maarten in Dutch), St. Eustatius, and Saba, comprising the Windward Islands of the Netherlands Antilles, are intermixed with the British "Leewards." Columbus christened St. Martin after the Catholic Saint Martin of Tours. Eustatius and Saba appear to be phonetic translations of their Indian names. As the log of those first sightings reveals, Columbus obviously saw a large part of the Caribbean in a very short time; his brief tour allowed no time for exploration.

Columbus's landfall was Dominica on his second voyage, but he only sailed around its northern end before heading for other islands in the distance. Anchoring off Guadeloupe on November 4, 1493, he sent a small exploratory party ashore, which got lost in the dense growth and took six days to find its way back to the coast. Columbus then proceeded northward on November 10, unsuspecting of the Carib encounter that lay ahead of him four days later on St. Croix. On the way he made a rough map relating the positions of the numerous Leeward Islands as he discovered them. Subsequent adventurers attempted to collate his map to reality, with the unfortunate result that some names were switched. St. Martin and Nevis, for example, are probably not the islands so named by Columbus.

The Spaniard Alonso de Ojedo, operating under the auspices of Amerigo Vespucci, technically discovered Aruba, Bonaire, and Curaçao in 1499. Although Italian, Vespucci (like Columbus) was sailing for Spain. Unlike Columbus, he published reports calling his discoveries a new continent and a "New World." Columbus did not dispute Amerigo Vespucci's claim and the Spanish mainland became known as "America." Dutch activity in the Caribbean is-

A touch of Paris crowns a cloud-draped hillside in Balata, Martinique, near Fort de France. Amid coconut palms and breadfruit trees, this scaled-down version of Sacré-Coeur calls to mind the island's French heritage.

lands just off the coast of Venezuela intensified in the early sixteenth century. A seafaring trading country needed expanded markets and Holland, through wealth brought in by her merchants, was becoming a very powerful state. Her New World activities ultimately included six Caribbean islands in addition to her colony of New Amsterdam, later to become New York.

Spain moved in to claim Curaçao in 1527, but the few settlers could not face the staunch competition from Holland's men and ships and fled to South America. By 1634, the Dutch had Curaçao to themselves; from this base, they spread to Aruba and Bonaire. Pirates were their chief rivals for the next century. Located near the treasure routes from South America, the trio of islands was a natural hideaway for the predators. Throughout those uncertain years, the Dutch never relinquished their claims. Except for the period of British control during the Napoleonic Wars from 1805 to 1816, the Dutch have ruled the three islands continuously. Soil and climate here were not favorable to serious agricultural development. The ABC's (as they came to be called) could never be "sugar islands." But a salt-pond evaporation enterprise did prosper under the unyielding sun and the diligent Dutch West India Company. A new installation on Bonaire now promises to boost exports to 500,000 tons of salt a year.

On Curaçao, an island just off the coast of South America, Dutch colonists erected buildings that looked as if they had been transported whole from Amsterdam. The islanders maintained close ties with their homeland, developing stable government and social institutions. The relative political calm of Curaçao attracted the installation of massive refineries for Latin American oil.

The discovery of fantastic oil reserves in Venezuela transformed them into a vital area. Three factors worked to bring the group a share of Venezuela's wealth—the islands are nearby (Aruba is only 15 miles offshore); they have good, protected harbors, and the stability of the Dutch government was appreciated in this area of political uncertainty. A subsidiary of Standard Oil of New Jersey built the largest refinery in the world on Aruba; and Shell Oil, the second largest, on Curaçao. Today, much of North America and Europe runs on oil drilled in Venezuela and refined in the Netherlands Antilles.

Willemstad, Curaçao, is one of the most colorful towns in the entire chain of islands. A local explanation is that an old governor thought white buildings hurt his eyes and so decreed a tax on them. Overnight, Willemstad became a pastel community, with a cheerful array of now much-photographed shops along the quay. Aruba, to the west, is interesting with its giant cactus fences, boulders of diorite, herds of eager goats, and spacious, domed limestone caves on the northern shore. Arawak, who used these natural rooms for their early homes, decorated the stone walls with red hieroglyphs, some of which remain. Bonaire, the most easterly island in the group, is quiet, peaceful, and somewhat isolated. Inland grottos still preserve Indian drawings. In Great Salt Lake there are flocks of giant, beautifully pink, long-legged flamingoes. Fishing and diving add to the available diversions.

About 1631 Holland also established a post on St. Maarten. Still trying to eject any intruders, the Spaniards recaptured the island in 1633—but the determined Dutch colonized St. Eustatius in 1636, Saba in 1640, and St. Maarten, for the second time, in 1648. Settlement attempts were also made on other islands but most of them ultimately became a part of the British Virgins.

Saba is a single volcanic cone jutting straight up from the sea. Breakers surrounding its sheer circumference must have discouraged all but the hardiest colonists. All five square miles of Saba culminate at the peak of Mt. Scenery, 2,910 above sea level. By carving a walkway directly into the mountainside, the enterprising settlers solved their unique transportation problem in a logical, if laborious, fashion. Before the first jeep arrived in 1947, only a "step road" of 800 rock treads connected Fort Bay and Windwardside.

Even as seemingly formidable an island as Saba had to be defended. After Henry Morgan's uncle successfully plundered St. Eustatius and Saba in 1665, a "falling rocks" defense was instituted. This system, used to repulse buccaneer attacks in 1688 and 1690, was an outgrowth of the terrain. Heavy rocks were piled onto planks spanning the narrow step passes. By pulling on ropes attached to the planks, a mini-avalanche could be released to roll down toward the attacking raiders.

Since nearby St. Eustatius was the commercial and administrative center for the two islands, each new owner assumed that Saba was included in the conquest. The tiny island technically changed hands about 12 times; but usually, no one arrived to take control, so the Sabians would carry on as usual.

Today modern transportation is opening Saba to the outside world. One edge of the rock barely accommodates a 1,300-foot runway for the daily Winair flights to St. Eustatius and St. Maarten. After 300 years of beaching all imports onto rocks in the breakers and then "heading" them up the "step road," the islanders will at last have their first dock at Fort Bay. Saba's nearly 1,000 inhabitants (most are named "Hassel" or "Johnson") are just beginning to feel that the rest of the world knows they exist.

Saba is a joy to visit. Hall's Gate used to be an almost isolated community on the island. Now it is the first settlement reached after dozens of hairpin curves up from the airport. There is a striking quality immediately apparent at every turn—everything is neat, exceedingly neat. Rows of spotlessly clean frame houses climb the hillside. Around their universally red-painted roofs, delicately hand-carved eaves decorations give evidence of the pride the owners take in their diminutive dwellings and the care they lavish on them. Yards and streets are maintained with a fastidiousness that even surpasses that of meticulous Dutch cousins on the Continent. Around the hills, Windwardside and Bottom, the other communities, appear to be dollhouse villages arranged by a loving proprietor. In the best tradition of positive thinking, Saba's license-plate slogan for her few automobiles boasts—"Saba, Unspoiled Queen."

Father Jean Baptiste Labat arrived in the West Indies near the turn of the eighteenth century and his remarkable *Memoirs* provides the most complete observations on Caribbean colonial life. Visiting Saba in 1701, the Catholic priest found the people living in a *"grande union"* where everyone cooperated, often taking meals together, and even killing animals in turn, each family using what it needed. The homes he described as "clean, well-cared for, gay and commodious." Shoemaking was then the major industry; the priest bought several pairs, duly noting their quality in his journal.

By 1781 there were about 150 families living self-sufficiently from shipbuilding, shoemaking, fishing, and agriculture. In 1850 the population had expanded to 1,661, but the economy had centered on agriculture. When abolition came in 1863, the islanders used an interim Dutch plan; slaves were to continue their work for ten years on a paid basis.

Toward the end of the century, Saba became an "Island of Women," for with sugar and indigo gone, the men found it necessary to work as sailors. Because they sent back money to the women and children, the people were ultimately called the "remittance so-

Pineapple, a botanical discovery of Columbus's voyages to the "Indies," is now grown throughout that Asian world he never reached.

ciety." About that time Gertrude Johnson returned from a Caracas boarding school run by Spanish nuns, bringing with her a special form of needlework, which the lonely women rapidly learned. There was a demand for this elaborate "fancy" or "Spanish work," especially in the United States. In 1907 exports of Spanish work reached 712 florins in local currency. By 1928, the peak year, the shipments amounted to 22,690 florins, a considerable total for the small island. Exports declined as the generation of women with sufficient patience to do the intricate work disappeared. A few ladies still do the embroidery on Irish linen, predominately for sale to tourists. It makes a unique purchase from an unusual island.

St. Eustatius, commonly called "Statia," has a colorful history. This barren island, too small for serious sugar production, seized upon an untapped commercial possibility to become the "Golden Rock" of the Caribbean. The Dutch saw the advantages of operating a port where flags of all nations would be welcome and a huge variety of goods available. They knew the Caribbean colonists could not resist trading, even though their mercantilist home governments forbade the exchange.

Soon, English and French planters were sending their sugar to Statia for transshipment to America and Europe. Statia moved 9,000,000 pounds of the confection in 1770; the figure had grown to 25,000,000 pounds by 1779. It was in this period that Jamaica and Statia became the most important slave markets in the Western Hemisphere, with most of the Africans going to North America. On some days as many as two hundred ships lay in the bay off Oranjestad. Sea communication via Statia was so brisk and dependable that Benjamin Franklin routed his correspondence to Europe through the Dutch colony.

The "Golden Rock's" fortunes were still rising on November 16, 1776, when an armed merchantman, the *Andrew Doria,* sailed into the roadstead and dipped the Great Union flag of the newly declared United States of America. The officer on shore in Fort Oranje acknowledged this by a similar dip of the fortress flag. The ship then fired a gun-salute. The fort responded in kind. As President Kennedy later noted in a telegram to Queen Juliana of the Netherlands, it was the first salute given by a foreign government to a flag flown by a United States vessel. For Statia this polite recognition would prove disastrous.

Tensions between England and the Netherlands over Statia had been growing for years. The British felt wronged by the illegal trade flourishing there. The salute of a warship from the colonies in North America that had just presumptuously declared their independence was too much for the English to accept. It took five years to arrive at the appropriate time for revenge, but when retribution came, it was unmerciful and thorough.

Admiral George Rodney was stationed in Barbados when he

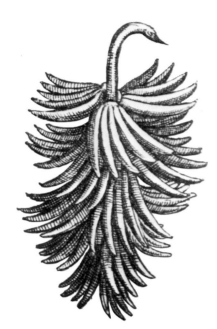

Bananas, an Asian fruit noted by Alexander the Great during his visit to India, were given a new home by European colonists in the West Indies.

received word that England had declared war on the Netherlands in December, 1780. Wasting no time, he raced his fleet to Statia before she got the news. The garrison of just 60 troops had no choice but to capitulate to Rodney's ultimatum. He took every ship lying in the roadstead and proceeded to sack the island. Since a conquering admiral customarily kept a percentage of the booty, Rodney carried away everything of value—goods then worth roughly $11,000,000. To compound the viciousness of the action, he dressed his men in Dutch uniforms and kept the Dutch flag flying over the fort for a month, a deceit that enabled him to capture some 150 more ships that had come to trade.

Statia was not ruined by this tragedy, as is often reported. Prosperity returned and by 1790 the population exceeded 8,000. However, the elaborate brick warehouses which lined the shore crumbled after a protective sea wall was destroyed. As the vigorous new United States of America developed its own commerce and England ended slave trading in 1807, Statia's usefulness diminished. Through-trade shipping to other countries was not as important as Europe's interminable wars paused after Napoleon. By 1816 Statia's population declined to 2,600. Today that number has dropped to about 1,200. Oranjestad resembles a ghost town, with about as many ruins as new buildings. A newly paved airstrip, a hotel, and some home construction are providing renewed hope for some development and new prosperity. But at present conveniences are still meager and visitors scarce.

St. Maarten's unusual feature is its binational division. The Dutch colonized it in 1648, followed closely by a French force from St. Kitts. After a small skirmish on Poincy's Heights, the two groups reached an amicable settlement. A treaty drawn up on March 23, 1648, and signed by both parties agreed that the French would have the part of the coast facing Anguilla to the northwest; the Dutch would have the southern section; both countries would share the salt ponds; the island would remain neutral in case France and the Netherlands went to war; and there would be a joint defense if the island were attacked. Though transgressed numerous times, the treaty has been remarkably durable. Both France and the Netherlands occasionally ruled the island alone, and Britain even gained control once; but the original terms were revived whenever the political upheavals of the day had passed.

Recently, a busy St. Maarten contractor was forced to run a midsummer ad expressing regret that he could not accept additional work for the balance of the year. The full-fledged construction industry has added a jet airport, resort houses, several condominiums, and elaborate hotels on the beaches, complete with golf course, casino, pools, and tennis courts. No entry or customs formalities hamper the tourist. Branches of fancy boutiques on St. Thomas and Curaçao offer duty-free shopping bargains.

Philipsburg is the typically neat, very Dutch, capital of St. Maarten. Situated on a sand spit between two hills, it is straining at its confined area between the ocean and the salt pond. An ambitious redevelopment project is under way; dredging and filling at the edge of the pond will double the available land and increase the number of city streets from two to four. New stores, government buildings, and apartments should ease the shortages now felt because of the rapid expansion.

Officially, only the different spelling on the roadside sign notifies the visitor he has passed into St. Martin, the French half of the island. Although there are no border formalities, the feeling of transition is there. The lilt and pace of life turn Gallic, chins tilt in a different way, and quick hand gestures subliminally suggest a spot in the south of France.

Marigot, the capital of St. Martin, has about 6,000 of the island's 13,000 people. Nestled around a harbor with water so clear that even the bottom rocks are discernible, Marigot has not yet participated in the prosperity now enjoyed by her neighbor. A few hotels entertain some guests, but most visitors see St. Martin by means of a day trip from the Dutch side.

The island's newest tourist attraction was never meant to be a curiosity. Envisioned as a fabulous hotel complex, La Belle

Dry, bleak, Dutch-owned St. Eustatius had no future as an agricultural investment. Holland transformed the tiny isle into a great trading center by opening the port to ships of all countries. Although legally barred by their governments from commerce with foreigners, Caribbean colonists welcomed the chance to buy, sell, and transship through Statia. A vigorous marketplace, the little island became the "Golden Rock of the Caribbean."

Creole dominates the peninsula separating ocean from bay. The grand design specified a complete Mediterranean village with courtyards, fountains, gardens, and plush rooms. Money poured into the project as buildings started to go up and handmade furniture arrived from Spain. Then, finally, the money ran out and the building stopped. La Belle Creole is a mere shell of walls, incompletely decorated with a few lights and ornately carved Spanish chairs. It never opened. As if prevented by voodoo, no people came. The village, too, stands empty now, and untrimmed flowers and vines run wild over the resort that never greeted guest.

St. Barthélemy (St. Barts), one of the least known French islands, is located about 15 miles southeast of St. Maarten. Its eight square miles and population of 2,500 are administered as part of the Department of Guadeloupe. Gustavia, the capital, surrounds its near-perfect harbor with an extraordinarily easy air. The absence of customs and a casual attitude make St. Barts a liquor buyer's paradise. No cheaper prices exist anywhere, and island schooners from throughout the Caribbean make regular visits. Many a wise yachtsman puts in to replenish his stores with French food and wines, as well as other bargain supplies that may be in stock.

Rock-strewn St. Barts had to be cleared before it could be farmed. European fence-building traditions gave the land its most striking visual characteristic: arrow-straight stone walls that divide the land with geometric perfection. The shoulder-high partitions stand perfectly formed without mortar, a tribute to the skill, patience, and pride of the earlier farmers.

In contrast to almost every other Caribbean island, where the descendants of slaves make up the present population, the ancestors of the people of St. Barts were principally either Swedish or French. Away from town, women still wear long turn-of-the-century black dresses and starched bonnets typical of Normandy and Brittany. Sweden administered St. Barts between 1784 and 1877, and blond, blue-eyed children are proof of their residency.

Exploration of the now-French islands began November 3, 1493. For his second voyage Columbus had rechristened the flagship from *Santa Maria* to *Mariagalante,* or "Gallant Mary." He named the first land he touched for his ship. This small isle, translated by the French to *Marie-Galante,* lies off Guadeloupe's (pronounced Gua-day-LOOP) southern coast.

As the Spaniards neared Guadeloupe's big mountain, historian Nicolo Syllacio later wrote, "Guadeloupe held the seamen close in its spell, with its wide and beautiful plains and the indescribable beauty of its mountains." Suddenly the men noticed something white coming down from the cloud-topped mountain. Columbus noted what appeared to be "a bridal veil from the sky." Dr. Chanca, chronicler of the voyage, wrote, "Many wagers were laid in the ships; some said it was white rocks and others said that it was

water." Then the ships moved close enough for all to identify the object of their fascination—a twin cascade tumbling hundreds of feet into a mossy rock-lined pool! Dr. Chanca recorded, "It was the fairest thing in the world to see from what a great height it fell and from how small a space so great a waterfall arose."

The first of many great shocks awaited Columbus as his men landed at Sainte Marie. He had been told the year before that strange Indians lived in these islands. Although he would not yet see any face to face, evidences of their presence horrified and frightened him. Cuts of human limbs hung in the abandoned huts, and two castrated Arawak boys and a dozen "very beautiful and very fat" girls were rescued from the village before they could be eaten. Even the brutal Spaniards had no heart for an encounter with people who ate their captives. Columbus stayed only long enough for Syllacio to note, "Their houses were built of thick reeds interlaced in the form of canopies; we were moved to admiration by their elegance."

Spain tried for years to colonize Guadeloupe but, unable to overcome the Caribs, gave up in 1604. As other European nations continued to encroach on Spain's territory, France rapidly moved in to lay claim to large, desirable islands, and in 1635 she sent colonists to settle in Guadeloupe. England quickly disputed their

Long French ownership and strong cultural ties turned Martinique into the most continental island in the Caribbean. Traditions and social order were saved by a quirk of history. Britain briefly had control of the land during the tragic period of the French Revolution which brought death to the upper classes on other islands. Martinique's elite were thus spared.

title and attacked them many times, finally seizing the island during the Seven Years' War (1759–1766). France soon regained it and maintained control until the French Revolution, when Britain sought to take all the islands owned by France. During the War of 1793, with so much energy diverted to the mother country, France lost Martinique, St. Lucia, and Guadeloupe, but before long sickness had taken a heavy toll of the victorious British troops.

At this point begins one of the grisliest sagas of Caribbean history. Carrying papers appointing him the new governor of the captured island, Victor Hugues, a repulsive trader from Haiti, arrived at Guadeloupe with an army on board his ships. As he approached land, he unveiled the glistening symbol of the Revolution, a guillotine mounted amidships. His 1,500 troops easily overpowered the weakened British garrison. Then, showing no mercy, Hugues started to behead the surrendered Royalists in the central square (where the annual carnival celebration is now held). This proved to be too slow a method to satisfy a madman, whereupon he ordered the French colonists buried alive! The French Revolution had come to the islands.

Slaves were liberated, plantation owners killed, and work abandoned. Since chaos persisted, Hugues forced the former slaves back to the fields, deeming them emancipated but not free to be idle. He continued to rule Guadeloupe by the guillotine until 1798, when he was tricked onto a boat bound for France. To his own amazement, the unnerved Hugues was entertained like a favorite and given a new assignment in Cayenne, French Guiana.

After Britain's victory at Waterloo in 1814 came the peace conference in Vienna. In return for other concessions, England renounced all claims to Guadeloupe. Sweden had nominal ownership in 1813, but France took permanent possession in 1816. One profound legacy of the French Revolution is that no real landed aristocracy exists on Guadeloupe as it does on Martinique, which escaped the guillotine's fury.

Guadeloupe is really two islands (Grande-Terre to the east and Basse-Terre to the west) separated by Rivière Salée, a small salty channel. Dominated by Mt. Soufrière, volcanically formed Basse-Terre boasts Guadeloupe's most spectacular scenery. From the sea level capital city, also called Basse-Terre, an arduous drive upward winds through the new 60,000-acre Natural Park, a heavily forested botanical treasure. Tropical flora along the road gives way to bubbling sulfurous banks, steam vents, and crusty yellow rocks. Near the top of Soufrière (4,813 feet), the pavement ends suddenly, as if defeated by the struggle against ascent and vegetation. That which was so lush and green is diminished to low bushes reminiscent of the Scottish moors. An occasional wild raspberry adds a dash of color to the muted scene. Chilling cloud-laden winds churn overhead, rumble between the passes, and press upon the valleys below. Pastel-painted Basse-Terre, 4,800 feet below, lazes in the warm Caribbean sun. This quiet panorama belies the volcano's stormy past, since a crop-destroying eruption occurred in 1797.

On the opposite side of the mountain awaits the waterfall that drew Columbus's initial attention to Guadeloupe. Chutes du Carbet is one of the great natural attractions in the Antilles, and getting there is much of the fun of seeing it. The paved road ends inside the Natural Park, where a new trail offers a moderately difficult but highly rewarding half-hour walk. The path twists and undulates through a virgin rain forest, with tree ferns and cecropia arched handsomely above. Heliconia, bromeliads, orchids, and philodendron brighten the damply matted way. Two footbridges lift the path across the waterfall's stream, to its end in a semicircular clearing enveloped in the steady roar and mist from Carbet's 700-foot plummet.

The other half of Guadeloupe contains the airport and the commercial center of Pointe-à-Pitre, with its 50,000 residents. Constantly crisscrossing the harbor, colorful schooners conduct their brisk island trade. Traditionally, flatter Grande-Terre has been intensively cultivated. Sugarcane fields still cover most of the island and account for much of the 175,000 metric tons shipped yearly. In contrast, the more rugged Basse-Terre is planted in sugar only on the lower slopes and in bananas at higher elevations.

From Pointe-à-Pitre a road leads southeastward to the popular beach areas. Long unbroken stretches of white sand reach past

England and France sparred over numerous West Indian islands. After several wars, and a few unsuccessful peace negotiations, the decisive Battle of the Saintes occurred south of Guadeloupe in 1782. Admiral Rodney and his British fleet met France's Comte de Grasse near the tiny French islands. The bloody struggle saw Rodney improvise unconventional fighting tactics, which broke France's sailing line and established England as undisputed Queen of the Caribbean.

At times even the elements seemed to conspire against the European settlers. Hurricanes, gigantic revolving tropical storms, roared in without warning to blow down and wash away years of work.

Gosier toward Sainte Anne with its restaurants and resort hotels. Some local bars gladly include free rum in the price of a set-up. Grande-Terre also offers moderately good French shopping, with wines, cheeses, patés, and perfumes selling for near-Paris prices.

For administrative purposes Guadeloupe oversees several other French islands. In addition to St. Barts and St. Martin, her dependencies include Marie-Galante, La Désirade, and Îles des Saintes. This latter group of small islands off Guadeloupe's southern shore witnessed a historic struggle.

On April 8, 1782, the fleets of England and France fought the decisive Battle of the Saintes from which Britannia emerged as mistress of the Caribbean. A conflict had actually been brewing for some time before England went to war against France and Spain. Admiral Rodney, stationed at St. Lucia, had kept lookouts posted atop Pigeon Hill to watch French activity on nearby Martinique. Admiral Comte de Grasse decided to move his fleet from Fort Royal (now Fort-de-France) to rendezvous with a Spanish squadron and form a superior force. The chase was on and continued northward past Dominica.

De Grasse turned back to help a French ship damaged in a collision. Rodney seized the opportunity and attacked. The battle began according to the classic plan, with two parallel lines of ships ready to fire as they sailed past each other. Suddenly a wind shift created a gap in the French line. The British hesitated only momentarily before boldly sailing through. Six ships took part in this new naval technique of "breaking the line," and the unorthodox procedure subjected the French to fire from two sides. When De Grasse struck his colors and surrendered to Rodney, 400 of his 1,300 flagship troops lay dead. Britain's sea power in the Antilles was never again seriously challenged.

Columbus attempted landing on Martinique during his fourth and final voyage in 1502, but the Carib sally from shore was so arrow-filled that he left without even naming the island. The Indian name *Madinina*, meaning "Island of Flowers," remained for years. No serious attempt to colonize Martinique was made until 1635, when Pierre Belain d'Esnambus landed and claimed it for France. Although the Caribs resisted to the end, they were completely exterminated by 1658. Except for two brief periods of British occupation, the island has been exclusively French ever since; a king's bargaining made it so.

During the negotiations for the Treaty of Paris in 1763, Louis XV traded Canada (calling it "a few snowy acres") and French interests in North America to England, rather than give up the French West Indies. This effectively eliminated French pressure around Britain's colonies on the mainland to the north. The king's move emphasized the importance Europe placed on West Indian agriculture.

When France left its islands relatively undefended to concentrate more attention on the problems of the Revolution, Britain occupied Guadeloupe and Martinique. The British administration of Martinique until 1801 spared the island's aristocracy from Hugues's blood-stained guillotine but little affected their day-to-day existence. Six leading families grew even richer as the plantations remained the core of the island's economic and social life.

The English captured Martinique once again during the Napoleonic Wars. When the French returned in 1814, the planters were thoroughly alienated from the entirely new government and social order which had developed in Paris, and they were part of a world that Parisians barely acknowledged. So the owners turned "inward," reinvested their money on the island, and looked upon Martinique as their permanent home. It is impossible to overemphasize the importance of this background when comparing Martinique to other islands where the majority of the plantations were held by absentee landlords.

Frenchness is the milieu of Martinique, most European of all Caribbean ports. Practically uninterrupted association with France has maintained a stability, orderliness, and cultural tradition that is unmatched in the West Indies. Martinique probably best portrays a European's notion of a proper West Indian island. It is beautiful and loyal, with resources, resolution, and a charming touch of the motherland's culture nicely blended with its own. History has, in many ways, been kind. Existence assumed a free and liberal character—bonds between planter and former slave, manager and laborer, broke racial lines and created a society that knows every conceivable color of skin. It is a comment on the French attitude toward their holdings, as well as on the beauty of the Martiniquais, that the island produced no fewer than six European queens, the most famous of whom was Empress Joséphine.

Marie Joséphine Rose Tascher de la Pagerie, the beautiful daughter of a French planter, reportedly was born in 1763 across the bay from Fort-de-France in the small village of Les Trois Îlets. At 17 she wed a fashionable Parisian viscount, only to be widowed by the Revolution. She married Napoleon in 1796, but he sadly divorced her in 1809 because she had not produced a male heir. Remaining true to their love, Joséphine continued to wait for his return on a small estate outside Paris until her death in 1814.

During the colonial period of sugar estates, St. Pierre, on Martinique's northwest Caribbean coast, grew to be a charming and gracious city. Often called "Little Paris," it held most of the island's social and economic life. Unfortunately, it lived in the shadow of Mont Pelée. One of the great tragedies of this century began to brew in April 1902 when the volcano started belching dust and pebbles. The citizens were interested but not unduly alarmed, although Pelée continued to broadcast its signals. The

An uncommon but deadly threat was eruption by any of the several volcanoes in the region. The most destructive tragedy occurred in 1902 when Mont Pelée obliterated the entire city of St. Pierre and its 30,000 inhabitants. This photograph, taken three weeks after the horror, is witness to the tremendous forces at work beneath the island chain.

end came suddenly on Thursday, May 8, 1902, when the whole side of Mont Pelée split apart. Enveloped by a 90-mile-per-hour inferno, St. Pierre and its 30,000 inhabitants vanished. The volcano continued to rumble for four more months and killed another 1,500 people in August. Since then, it has been relatively quiet.

Seventy years later much of St. Pierre is still shattered. Fragmented stone walls outline the ruins of ocean-front buildings. Marble segments once part of elaborate columns lie where they rolled. A nude figure, carved from volcanic rock to memorialize the catastrophe, lifts herself above the rubble. People were afraid to resettle in the path of destruction, and St. Pierre's functions were assumed by Fort-de-France.

Other aspects of life on Martinique have not been so somber. Napoleon was not the only Frenchman to find the island's women especially attractive. Before moving to Tahiti, Paul Gauguin, the French Impressionist painter, lived south of St. Pierre and wrote enthusiastically of the "sweet, soft-eyed sentimental country girls." A later writer described the appealing mulattoes as "straight as palms, supple and tall, with a dignified carriage and an easy elegance of movement." Most visitors take notice and agree. Dressed in the latest Parisian fashions, Martinique girls move with a grace and bearing all their own. Creamy-skinned shopgirls may be speaking the same language as their mainland counterparts, but they do it with a style and sparkle that are strictly local. Girl-watching, superb along the downtown streets, comes into full flower at the city's popular cafés. The long-lunch crowd lingers to savor the sights, sounds, fragrances, and sweet society that mingle here.

Drinking is in the French style, with a little "island" added. The leisurely lunch period and early evening are peak hours in the open-air cafés. Typically, a large glass brimming with rum and topped with a lime slice is downed straight and followed by a bottled-water chaser. Sometimes customers mix their own punch at the table—rum added to sugarcane syrup with just a dash of lime.

The British West Indies have their cricket, but soccer (or "football," as the Europeans call it) is the French Antilles passion. Teams turn out at 5:00 A.M. in Joséphine's Park in Fort-de-France to follow a well-organized morning regimen until they must stop so that work can begin. As soon as the offices close, the park is again filled with simultaneous matches that continue, amid heated audience participation, until dark.

The French and Dutch Antilles are more closely allied with their homelands than any other Caribbean islands. Being departments of France, and, therefore, a part of Europe, Guadeloupe and Martinique have the same customs duty, money, police, and military protection as Paris. A banana stem grown in Guadeloupe enters the French economy, or the European Common Market, just as a bottle of Burgundy wine. The Netherlands Antilles operates its own local government centered in Curaçao. Representatives are elected from the six islands to the *Staten*, which handles all affairs, in effect, except foreign and defense. Appointed by the ruling political party, a member is sent to The Hague to represent the Antilles in Holland's Parliament. The Dutch islands have their own currency and customs department with goods from Holland subject to some duty. Since maintenance of officials in the Windwards group would cost more than the collections would net, there are no customs. If the islands contribute additional work to imported manufactured materials, the products can be exported to Holland without duty. Thus, Venezuela's oil refined in Aruba and Curaçao can enter the Netherlands and the Common Market at a favorable price, even though the Dutch islands are only associated with the Common Market. Both groups contrast with the former British West Indies which, except for Commonwealth concessions, are faced with world price competition for the products.

An intriguing phenomenon is the intense social legacy provided by France. Wherever she stepped, she left a characteristic imprint of language and culture. Even islands which have not been under her domination for over a century retain substantial and observable Frenchness. In the French Antilles, almost continually administered by Paris, the flavor is complete in all facets of life,

Fiery European sentiment against slavery during the nineteenth century was fanned by several outspoken writers who raised the public's interest to the point of action. Victor Schoelcher was an Alsatian deputy and leading French abolitionist. His impassioned writings on the Martinique slavery conditions are credited with freeing 72,000 blacks there in 1848. A small town on the island's leeward coast and the Fort-de-France library honor his name. The Creole costume remained in vogue with Martinican women and survives as a national symbol.

from the breakfast *croissant* to the streetcorner *gendarme*. Others think of themselves as "islanders"—a St. Vincentian considers himself a "St. Vincentian," not a "Briton"; but a Martinican is unequivocably and irrevocably a Frenchman.

Holland's cultural impression, although not as definite, is certainly discernible. There is a pride and acceptance of citizenship which is really quite appealing. The Dutch islander, besides being unalterably neat, maintains a friendly, law-abiding attitude toward human relations, a careful and deliberate approach to his work.

Caribbean ties with France and Holland actually grow stronger all the time, in large part because those who can afford it seek European schooling and often marry European girls. Both the French and Dutch islands have happily and successfully incorporated ideas from distant lands and diverse populations within their framework of government, to preserve and blend the several elements of their heritage.

Saba's dramatic landscape rises directly from the sea to culminate in one massive volcanic cone, Mt. Scenery. Succeeding in an arduous task, Sabians hand-carved a cross-island road from solid rock to open their 4.8-square-mile homeland to vehicular traffic. The tenacious Dutch citizens now attract tourists with their newly built airport and dock.

THE DUTCH & FRENCH ANTILLES

Trimmed hedges, fretwork eaves, and red-painted roofs greet the visitor to the tiny world of Saba. Dutch in government, English in language, the island is surprisingly cosmopolitan in its outlook—thanks to the wide travels of its seafaring men. Etched into the faces of two former merchant fleet captains are years of bridge watch on all the seas of the world. Forced abroad by the limited economic horizons of their volcano birthplace, Sabian men return home to join their families for shore leave and retirement. Anchored into this precipitous Eden's five square miles are four villages—Windwardside, Hell's Gate, St. John's, and the Bottom.

Warehouse ruins crumbling into a relentless sea are ghostly reminders of St. Eustatius's elegant past. The "Golden Rock" was once the trading center of the Caribbean, its merchants offering treasures from every corner of the world. Admiral Rodney dealt "Statia" a disastrous blow by looting the island in retaliation for its recognition of and arms trade with the 13 British colonies in revolution to the north. The Dutch half of neighboring St. Maarten is today experiencing a growth in trade with those colonies—now the United States. Newly built hotels offer Americans *riijstaafel*, the Dutch smorgasbord originated during the days when the Netherlands ruled Indonesia. Japanese fishermen catch Caribbean tuna from their Philipsburg base, exporting to Japan and the United States.

Dutch St. Maarten's narrow capital of Philipsburg separates the Caribbean from a once profitable salt pond, originally utilized during the settlement of the island. A new reclamation plan will double the town's size by filling in some of the pond. The neatly ordered Dutch world is subtly contrasted as the traveler passes across an unguarded border to the more casual French side of the island. Here Gallic concern for life-style and Creole flair for languor blend into a special sweetness typical of the French Caribbean. High above a Marigot street, a boy's dreams are borne by elegant ironwork balcony supports, reminiscent of another French colonial effort, New Orleans. French and Dutch have shared this tiny island since 1648, enjoying a harmony that has fostered and encouraged diversity.

Much of the character of St. Barts today is directly related to the two countries that owned it. Sweden administered the island for almost a century. Her legacy is blond children like these, who are running past the old Swedish clock tower that stands above Gustavia, named for King Gustavus III. St. Barts was mainly settled from France's northern provinces, Normandy and Brittany. Native costumes from that region are still commonly seen on the older white residents of the island's smaller communities. The younger generation and visitors are much more likely to wear France's newer costume, the bikini. White sand beaches around the small dependency of Guadeloupe are uncrowded even in season. St. Barts's charm and beauty have made it a popular Caribbean hideaway for wealthy Americans and Frenchmen. Several daily interisland flights and absence of customs formalities simplify access.

Martinique's most famous citizen left the island to become France's most celebrated woman. Marie Rose Joséphine Tascher de la Pagerie, born in the village of Les Trois Îlets, fell in love with and married Napoleon Bonaparte in Paris. A statue of Empress Joséphine graces the heart of the capital, Fort de France. Ruins still lie in the center of St. Pierre, known as "Little Paris" before the disastrous eruption of Mt. Pelée in 1902. Thirty thousand residents perished in the gas, steam, and ash inferno; within a matter of minutes their city was reduced to rubble. Long-time curator of the local volcanic museum, Joseph Bonnet-Durival displays a bottle melted by the deadly heat.

Europe and Africa blended most completely and fluidly in the French islands, where blood and culture together wove a new Creole fabric. Bedecked in costumes that typified the combination, women indicated their disposition by their madras headdress. One point raised meant "My heart is free." Today's Martinican is more likely to wear an Afro hairdo, don the latest French fashions, and display her Creole heritage with earrings. Her perspective may be as mixed as the color of her skin—influenced by Paris schools and an island future. Martinique's economy relies on its "foreign port" appeal to attract tourist dollars. Unlike most other islands where the majority of visitors arrive by air, Martinique welcomes many arrivals from cruise ships.

Columbus steered toward a captivating land-
mark on Mt. Soufrière as he approached Chutes
du Carbet. Isolated high in Guadeloupe's new
Natural Park, the 700-foot waterfall has carved
its own amphitheatre. Club Méditerranée,
France's most popular vacation organization,
operates two resorts in the French islands. The
former Fort Royal luxury hotel is Guadeloupe's
casual group-fun center. Bikinis are the only
outfits needed for a week's sun-filled activities.
Buffets, sports equipment, and twice-daily wine
are included in the fixed-price package.

III.
DOMINICA & THE PLANTER ISLES

As the jumbled history of the Caribbean unfolds, some islands fall into natural groupings. Puerto Rico and Cuba, held by the Spanish principally for the defense of their treasure fleets, remained largely undeveloped for years. Other islands became useful almost exclusively for their cultivation of sugarcane. In the Leewards these planter isles were Antigua, Montserrat, Nevis, and St. Kitts. One island, Dominica, does not fit any category.

Dominica (pronounced Dom-i-NEE-ka) is a wonderland. Wild and untamed, with an aura of mystery, its tangled mass is much the same today as when fierce Caribs ranged its opulent slopes. The incredible terrain has kept it isolated. Morne Diablotin rises on the northern end of the 28-mile-long island to a height of 4,747 feet, one of the highest mountains in the Caribbean. Still, one peak does not tell the story. With almost no level ground, Dominica has been estimated to be more rugged per square mile than Switzerland. The airport was carved from a coconut tree plantation, and planes must make a mountaintop approach in order to land in a downhill roll toward the sea. The 90-minute taxi drive to Roseau, the capital, carries the visitor through some of the most beautiful mountain scenery in the tropics. As the road winds upward from the Windward coast, the jungle closes in until rich hanging greenery grazes the passing car. Lined with thickets of crackling bamboo, cascading streams tumble into cool river pools. Every turn offers a new botanical view.

This spectacular island remains unspoiled: the sole example of how much of the Antilles must have looked when the first Europeans arrived. Dominica is a study in greens. Approaching the island by sea, one notes the layered effect of green superimposed upon green, ascending the tiered hills to a rainbow-filled sky. Waterfalls spill from vine-draped cliffs, and hundreds of clear mountain currents fume toward the ocean far below. A naturalist's dream, Dominica is unforgettable.

Like so many of the other islands, Dominica was discovered and named by Columbus, who steered toward the mountain peaks on his second voyage in 1493. Dr. Chanca, the fleet surgeon, re-

A few rock carvings, such as these on St. Kitts, and the small number of "pure" Caribs on their Dominican reservation are the scant remains of a once dominant tribe. Though fierce, they were no match for the Europeans.

corded, "On the first Sunday after All Saints, namely the third of November, about dawn, a pilot on the ship *Capitana* cried out: 'The reward, I see the land.' All that part of the island which we could observe, appeared mountainous, very beautiful, and green, even up to the water, which was delightful to see, for at that season, there is scarcely anything green in our own country."

Columbus did not land but passed on to the north. When later Spanish explorers learned the extent and demeanor of Dominica's native population, they decided that Spain did not need another island badly enough to fight over one so staunchly defended. Other countries struggling to dominate the West Indies also had second thoughts about the battle risks on Dominica. Thus, the hurricane of conflict circled around the island, leaving it a relatively calm eye in the storm until the middle of the seventeenth century. Then France began to occupy desirable lands not held by the Spanish. Lying between Guadeloupe and Martinique, Dominica logically became a French colony. Although the French settlers stayed long enough to name most of the rivers, mountains, and points of interest, they never solved the problem of peaceful coexistence with the Caribs. Constant running battles were fought first with the Indians and then the British. For over a hundred years control of Dominica vacillated between England and France. In 1805 the dispute was resolved in favor of the British, who ruled the island until its recent entry as an Associated State of the West Indies.

Native Dominicans converse in a lilting *patois* more like singing than speaking. Their supple bodies move with a fluid grace that transforms even walking into a balanced rhythm—burdens of laundry and market are carried deftly atop native heads. Hard physical labor and an outdoor life have given them attractive physiques and robust good health. They do their washing and bathing in the generous rivers. Dominican children reflect the gentleness and friendliness of the people, for they are not only congenial among themselves but eager to meet the tourist as well. The older youngsters carefully look after the small ones, although a parent is never too far away if needed. Knowing no manufactured playthings, the children enjoy such universal toys as a broken wheel or sticks and stones. They will work for days fashioning a coaster to ride down the rocky hills.

Other islands are of interest because of their political history; Dominica is fascinating because of her natural history. Every excursion into the bush is a visual treat. A day's journey across the arduous backbone of ridges will provide a lifetime of tropical scenery. From the Caribbean Sea on the Leeward coast the road pushes upward through a slit in the jungle past huge saman trees, which majestically form a silhouetted canopy of leaves. Orchids and bromeliads of many varieties festoon almost every tree. The moist, richly organic perfume of nature delights the senses with its freshness and purity. An occasional orange or lime grove shows through

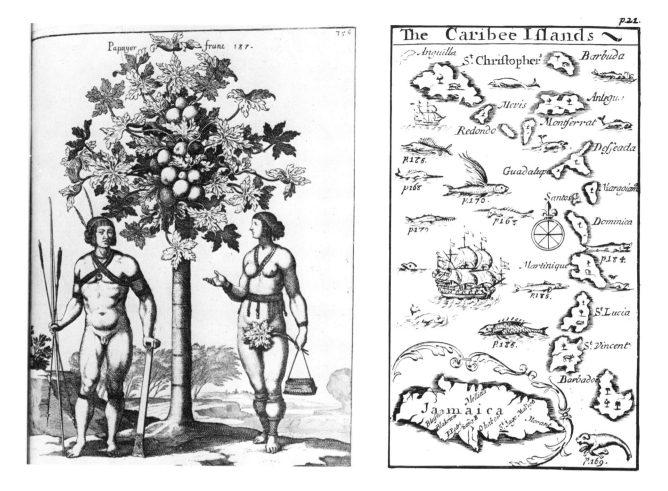

the thicket, but the main indication of civilization is the omnipresence of cultivated bananas.

Bananas overflow the slopes and cling so precariously to the cliffs that it is difficult to see how they grow there and impossible to understand how the fruit can be harvested. They are, however, the principal cash crop on Dominica. Men climb carefully through the narrow tropical paths to look for bananas ready for cutting. With stems of 50 pounds or more on their heads, the workers make their way down steep mountain trails to thatched way-stations along the highway. There the still-green fruit lies until open trucks carry them to boxing plants.

As in other islands contracted to Geest Industries, Ltd., the arrival of the familiar white refrigerator cargo ship signals "banana day." Beneath 30-pound burdens, women hold their heads in stately rigidity while their bodies move independently with the fluid abandon of the loading ritual. Sounds of their voices float gaily on the ocean breezes. Heavy banana boxes glide toward the sea on this supple human conveyor belt. By day's end, the week's harvest of more than 1,000 tons will be stowed in the ship's hold for the eight- to ten-day voyage to England. Often a loader will call out to a passing car, "Hey, man, you want ripe 'figs'?" She knows full well that these bananas will not be table-ready for another two weeks, when a

The Carib Indians lived a relatively peaceful and easy existence. A pleasant climate eliminated the need for clothes. Food was plentiful on the land and in the sea. Tended by their women, the men had few cares in their island Eden. But, once the tribe voted for battle, they transformed themselves into the cannibals feared by other Indians throughout the West Indies. A 1685 map illustrated the dimensions of a distant exotic world. Frontiers of their day, the "Caribee Islands" excited the imaginations of would-be adventurers.

London housewife will take them home for dinner.

Limes are the other crop grown beneath Dominica's peaks. In the nineteenth century scientists discovered that the scourge of scurvy could be prevented by serving citrus to the sailors, but without refrigeration fresh fruit spoiled on long sea voyages. The British firm of L. Rose and Company developed a secret technique for processing lime juice so that it would keep in wooden kegs below deck. Dominica became the principle supplier. Since Vitamin C is now provided in other ways, the company remains the largest employer on Dominica by producing Rose's Lime Juice, a popular cocktail mixer.

The serpentine road struggles against the slope, passing patches of bananas and jungle alternately on its way to Pont Cassé (affectionately called "Piccadilly"), a roundabout where four roads meet and the downhill drive to Castle Bruce begins. Not far beyond the circle, the jungle admits a small path, an unobtrusive invitation for adventure. Three steps off the asphalt take the traveler from roadside undergrowth to tropical rain forest. Giant boisdiable and chataignier trees are so entwined with philodendron that the noonday sun never reaches the ground. Winding downhill, the path leads precipitously past a sheer drop to the river below and Dominica's *grande scene*, Emerald Pool. A delicately picturesque waterfall cascades coolly into the white sand basin. Ferns, lianas, and mosses mantle the vaulted ledges and enormous boulders divert the silvery stream. The ardent romantic may not be able to resist a swim in the icy water.

Gigantic gommier trees stab over 150 feet into the mountain sky. Long before Columbus arrived, Caribs were hollowing canoes from single trunks of this dense golden wood. Each tree stands majestically apart like a sentry guarding the island's seclusion.

Geometrical rows of stately coconut palms line the sloping coastal hills. The fruit is harvested mainly for its copra, as the white meat is called after drying. When pressed, copra yields up to 65 percent of its weight in coconut oil, approximately one gallon from 30 nuts. This valuable island product lends Caribbean cooking its characteristic flavor and is also an ingredient in cosmetics, candles, and soaps. The remaining desiccated cakes, or "coconut stearins," are sold for cattle fodder and fertilizer. Practically nothing is wasted on a copra plantation. Palm trunks provide lumber, coconut milk makes delicious drinks, husks are the fuel for drying the coconut meat, and leaves and fibers are materials for roof thatch, placemats, baskets, and hats. The beneficent coconut is considered the most useful of all palm trees.

Ahead lies Castle Bruce and the windward coast. All nature's wild power seems converged for flamboyant display along this eastern shore. Waves "from Africa" pound the rocks, making the air vibrate in a never-ending soliloquy. Vegetation, bowing to the wind

Abolitionists' myths have so obscured reality that it is now difficult to determine the truth regarding slavery. There is no doubt that life for the blacks was a routine of long hot work and few weekend pleasures. The masters were usually anxious to punish all infractions, not only to set examples but to discourage even the possibility of a slave revolt. Still, there was some time for play. Sundays were often spent singing and dancing as oft-told stories of the good days in Africa were repeated once again for the children.

like the tresses of a mermaid, is bathed by spume and flung against the cliffs to dry. Each panorama is more breathtaking than the last, as dramatic bays form arcs of uninhibited beauty, relenting only to the raging surf.

It is ironic but fitting that the last of the Caribs find their home on this untamed coast. Since Dominica was declared neutral by France and England in 1748 and essentially left to the Caribs, Indians remained here after they had been exterminated on the other islands, but their reservation is small. Unfortunately, no definitive study of the tribe was ever made. Father Labat, on one of his many journeys, crossed Dominica to visit a Carib village. He later wrote that they did not, in fact, eat people regularly but merely "boucaned" some of their adversaries' meat, to have it around for festivals. Such may have been the case by 1700 in that particular group, but the overwhelming evidence is that Caribs boiled, roasted, and enjoyed human flesh regularly. They even specialized, preferring men and baby girls to women and boys, whom they found not too tasty. Looking back in the 1800s on his life with the Europeans, one old Carib reminisced that he thought the French were probably the tenderest people of all the Christians he had ever eaten.

Anthropologists believe that the Caribs probably originated in Brazil, canoeing from the northeastern tip of South America to Trinidad. Fighting was their way of life as they proceeded up the archipelago, taking female captives for new mates and eating male prisoners as they went. This horrible practice gave the world the new word *cannibal*. The Arawak name for the Caribs was *"Caniba,"* sometimes translated by the Spaniards as *"Caribal,"* which formed the basis for naming the cannibalistic tribe and their territories. The Caribbean Sea and its islands also carry their name, although the terrible connotation has long since faded in the brilliance of the tropical sun and the balm of moonlit nights.

The Arawak knew from firsthand experience of both the Caribs' cannibalism and their ferocity. Columbus chose discretion after his initial encounter with them at St. Croix, and avoided them whenever he could. The early settlers found themselves in constant conflict with the Caribs and often came out second best. Europeans called them lazy because most of the men spent their days lying in hammocks while the women groomed them. Once moved to action, however, the natives would proceed with single-minded determination, a trait that lead to an oft-quoted slogan of the time: "Cross a Carib and you have to fight him; fight him and you have to kill him." Which they did.

Although few pure Caribs remain, many of the people along the new unpaved road between Castle Bruce and Salybia have characteristics (straight black hair, high cheekbones, and reddish-brown skin) that indicate an Asian heritage. The 1960 census

FILET OF SNAPPER
Cook a small bunch of scallions in a shallow pan until tender. Bottom of pan should be covered with two tablespoons butter, two tablespoons coconut oil, and one tablespoon water. Add two snapper filets; one tablespoon each chopped bell peppers, celery, and parsley. Cover and simmer for ten to fifteen minutes. Remove fish to warm platter. Add to pan juices the juice of two green West Indian limes and ½ teaspoon paprika. Strain and pour over fish.

listed "395 Indians of Carib descent." Most of them have intermarried over the centuries to create what are today known as "Black Caribs." However, an occasional native still reveals enough "pure" features to satisfy the sightseer. It is difficult to reconcile the shyness of the contemporary Caribs with the fierce reputation of their ancestors. Most of these gentle people run to hide at the first sign of a camera, but smiles will sometimes coax cooperation.

The combination of Caribs and topography determined Dominica's progress. Unfit for cultivation, unsafe for civilized habitation, and unnecessary as a fortress site, the island appeared to possess a "fatal gift of beauty." Even the British Crown seemed to conspire against her. Although a public land sale in the eighteenth century offered most of the island in lot-sized parcels, not a penny of the million-dollar-profit was reinvested on Dominica. Instead, the money was used for Queen Charlotte's dowry.

Dominica has begun to awaken today; however, tourism will never thrive here as it has on the flatter islands, which more easily accommodate jet airstrips, beach-front hotels, and industrialization. Lovely little inns high in the rain forest and rental Volkswagens are about as far as her tourist boom has progressed.

The planter isles lie only a hundred miles away, but they are a world apart. The wild beauty of Dominica is sharp contrast to the cultivated manicure of centuries-old sugar plantations on Antigua, Montserrat, Nevis, and St. Kitts. Most visitors to this section of the Leeward group arrive first at Antigua (pronounced An-TEE-ga) because of the convenient air connections with the United States and Europe.

British planters from nearby St. Kitts first settled Antigua in 1632. With the exception of a single year of French rule in 1666, it remained an English island until it joined the Associated States of the West Indies in 1967. Antigua's early history was tied to the development of English Harbour, located on the southern coast. This was described in a 1671 letter to London from Antigua's governor as "so land locked as to be out of danger of hurricanes."

These huge storms represented a considerable threat to the Europeans, who had never experienced them on the Continent. *Hurricane* is an Arawak word, for these Indians also lived in dread of the destructive sea winds. Soon after colonization, the Europeans realized there was a pattern to the "big blows," and they put their shipping on alert during the late summer and early fall, when storms could be expected. What modern technology and "hurricane hunter" aircraft have learned about the winds would have saved the planters much misery and loss. For still unknown reasons, low pressure systems develop east of the Caribbean islands, particularly in August and September. High temperatures and high humidity are necessary for their growth. If the conditions are right, strong counterclockwise winds whirl around a small center, or "eye," and

PLANTERS' PUNCH
One of sour (one part fresh lime juice)
Two of sweet (two parts sugar)
Three of strong (three parts West Indian rum)
Four of weak (four parts water and ice)
Dash of Angostura bitters, stir well, serve in cold, tall glass.

Lord Horatio Nelson

the huge mass moves in a northwesterly direction. The eye is calm, and frequently no more than ten to fifteen miles across, but its edge is ripped by violent winds which sometimes reach up to 200 miles per hour. Many factors affect the speed, direction, and intensity of such a storm. Early settlers were completely at the mercy of the elements; by contrast hurricanes today are followed throughout their life-cycles and warnings are generally possible several days in advance through the use of data from airplanes, radar, and satellite photographs.

England's increased West Indian activities in the late seventeenth century created a great need for a safe harbor. She required facilities for refitting and supplying ships; Antigua provided the ideal site. Berkeley Fort was built in 1704 to protect the sea approaches to English Harbour, and the first British warship arrived in 1707. By the end of the eighteenth century, English Harbour was the busiest dockyard in the British Empire, a bustling station capable of performing almost any service required by the stream of ships stopping there.

Dashing young 26-year-old Captain Horatio Nelson, destined to be his country's most famous war hero, assumed his first command at English Harbour in 1784. Also serving there was the future King William IV, Prince William Henry, the Duke of Clarence, who had an attractive hillside cottage built across the water overlooking the harbor. (Gracious Clarence House is now used as a country residence for Antigua's Prime Minister.) Immediately impressed with Nelson, the Prince wrote, "He appeared to be the merest boy of a captain I ever beheld. . . . There was something pleasing in his address and conversation; and an enthusiasm when speaking on professional subjects, that showed he was no common being."

Unfortunately, what might have been one of the happiest times of Nelson's life turned into three years of miserable service. He was appalled at the amount of corruption in the dockyard—American vessels moved freely through English Harbour even though Britain expressly forbade trade with the United States following the Revolutionary War. In 1785 he wrote: "If once the Americans are admitted to any intercourse with these islands, the views of the Loyalists are entirely done away. . . . The residents of these islands are Americans by conexion [*sic*] and by interest, and are inimical to Great Britain. They are as great rebels as ever they were in America, had they the power to show it."

When Nelson tried to enforce the law, he only alienated the local citizens, who profited from the increased traffic. Lonely and friendless, he found companionship on nearby Nevis in the person of Frances Nesbit, a widow with a small son. They were married in 1787.

English Harbour is now being restored to its original condition. Reconstruction began in 1951 after a report to the Colonial

Office in London described the state of the dockyard as "deplorable." Blueprints for the original buildings were discovered in England, and local artisans were found who had the skills necessary for rebuilding the area by eighteenth-century construction procedures. Volunteers labored and visiting yachtsmen contributed, so that English Harbour now bustles with ships from around the world—bearing vacationers, not warriors and tradesmen.

In addition to their successful harbor, Antiguan colonists established a thriving sugar industry. Despite the varied fruits and vegetables native to the Caribbean (Columbus found yams, sweet potatoes, cinnamon, rhubarb, and pineapples), the area was developed as a single-crop economy. Modern visitors find it difficult to understand why eighteenth-century Europeans valued sugar so highly. Though abundant and inexpensive today, it was so important in the early history of the West Indies that the Antilles were commonly called the "Sugar Islands."

Sugar was first cultivated in India, then introduced to Europe during the Crusades. Rare and expensive as a spice, it was considered a luxury even by the rich. The Spanish started growing cane in the Azores and Canary islands, and were so successful that Columbus brought some plants with him to the isle of Hispaniola on his second voyage.

The dramatic growth of the Caribbean sugar industry resulted from three circumstances. First, the newly popular drinks of tea and coffee created strong demand for sugar among Europeans. Second, the Islands were just beginning to be successfully colonized, and the settlers were looking for cash crops to sell to Europe. Finally, the slave trade was operating along the African coast, and a large, pliable labor force became available to cultivate sugar in the tropics. Import figures illustrate how these circumstances combined into an explosive mixture that influenced world politics for over 300 years: In 1700 England consumed about 10,000 tons of sugar; by 1800 the figure had jumped to 150,000 tons; by 1880 the total leaped to over a million tons.

Sugar profits attracted both investment capital and more settlers. The development of each planter isle generally followed a similar pattern. Huge areas were cleared and planted with cane; and slave shacks were put up a quarter-mile from the main mill and downwind of the master's house. Shortly before sunrise, a blast from a conch shell roused the displaced Africans for their rigorous work day. While the men and the stronger women began in the fields, other slave women prepared a breakfast of seasoned local vegetables. Forty-five minutes were allowed for an eight o'clock breakfast while laggards on the early morning shift received the customary whipping. The work pace slowed as midday approached and the tropical sun bore heavily on the sweat-soaked workers, but a two-hour noon break for eating and sleeping put the slaves into a better mood for their long afternoon's work. This

Lord George Rodney

was the most productive period—muscles loosened in the oppressive heat and workers moved through the cane with an almost abandoned air. Old African songs and rhythms lightened the heavy blows of the driver's whip.

When the cane ripened, cutlass-wielding slaves slashed through the fields. The newly harvested cane was carried to the busy mills. (Their ghostly remains dot the island landscapes today.) Powered by wind, animals, or slaves, gigantic rollers inside the mills crushed the cane. The juice ran down through a pipe to the boiling room. Fires under blackened iron cauldrons kept the fluid near the boiling point as it progressed toward the last pot, where it arrived sufficiently concentrated to crystallize. Molasses was sometimes diverted to the nobler and equally lucrative manufacture of rum.

Although many planters turned profits large enough to make the phrase "rich as a West Indian" common in Europe, the sugar business never seemed to run smoothly. Military attacks from other islands were a constant danger, and work problems with the slave labor created great strains. Today, it is impossible to view the institution of slavery through the eyes of a seventeenth-century European. Prisoners of war throughout the world were often held in bondage. A slave was considered just a poor unfortunate who had lost his luck. There was no overriding moral examination of the system; that would take another three centuries. The first Africans were brought to the islands by a Spanish governor even before Columbus's last voyage. As the Indians refused to work and were killed off, Caribbean colonists turned to slaves as a necessary work force. The bitterness and resentment planted then still linger today, a regrettable legacy.

Barbuda, just over Antigua's northern horizon, was the site of an unheralded slave experiment. To provide a better worker stock and to establish a local supply of new laborers, large healthy black males waited here for the boats that brought African women to be impregnated. The object of this breeding was to produce a strain of "super slaves." From that standpoint, it was never a very successful project, but the usual tourist comment in response to the scheme is, "Well, at least they were able to have some fun."

An almost deserted flat rock fringed by 35 miles of uninhabited white beach, Barbuda is more obscure than most other Caribbees. Fishing and diving are superb. But the only hotel is so exclusive that, to discourage unregistered guests, it quotes $50 as the price for lunch. The entire island is government-owned and administered by Antigua. Barbudans are allowed to live just in Codrington, its single community. One-day trips are possible via LIAT Airlines from Antigua.

If Barbuda seems restful to the tired vacationer, Montserrat (pronounced Mon-ser-ROT) appears absolutely somnolent. Located 35 miles southwest of Antigua, the tiny island is so little

For most of the inhabitants of the planter isles, life centered around the sugar crop. The numerous slaves needed to work the fields lived physically near the plantation Great House, but their accommodations were downwind and distinctly different. To form a new crop small cuttings of stalk were planted, each with a joint, or "eye." When the cane was ripe enough to be cut it would be taken to giant windmill-powered crushers where the precious juice was mashed from the cane stalks. The juice then was boiled in great vats, the water evaporated, and the remaining liquid reduced to a thick sugar syrup. Huge hogsheads of the valuable sweetener, each weighing up to 1,500 pounds, were loaded for shipment and sale in the American colonies or to Europe.

75

known that it seems like a personal discovery to each visitor. It is the only Caribbean island to have an Irish heritage. Seeking a new life away from the English Protestants on St. Kitts, Irish-Catholics settled in 1632. The only traces of their presence are some spoken accents and the parish names, such as St. George's, St. Peter, and St. Anthony.

Called the "Garden Island of the West Indies," Montserrat still derives its support principally from agriculture. Tourism is not a large factor in the island's economy. Even during the winter months, hotel guests are outnumbered by part-time residents, mainly Americans and Canadians, who occupy their own vacation homes.

When Columbus first saw the island, he wrote that its velvety peaks suggested the Abbey of Montserrat outside Barcelona. The name endured though the Spanish did not. In 1664 the French gained control, beginning a period of transition that saw Montserrat administered by England, then France, and in 1783, by England once again. Too Lilliputian to risk independence, it remains as the smallest (32 square miles) British Crown Colony in the Caribbean with an administrator answering to the Queen.

Nevis (pronounced NEE-vis) lies just to the northwest of Montserrat. Here the lonely Horatio Nelson came courting and here he married. The Duke of Clarence, later to be the "Sailor King" (William IV), sailed over from the British naval station on Antigua to give the bride away. Although the master's house on Montpelier Estate, where the wedding took place, stands no longer, the record book of Fig Leaf Church near Charlestown still bears a faded notation of the event: "1787. March 11, Horatio Nelson, Esquire, Captain of his Majesty's Ship, the *Boreas*, to Frances Herbert Nesbit, Widow."

Now a member of the Associated States, Nevis was first colonized by British settlers from St. Kitts in 1688. With her fortunes always tied to St. Kitts because of the easy passage across the two-mile channel separating them, Nevis rapidly became a successful planter isle. Sacking it in 1706, a French fleet took 3,000 slaves and so devastated the island that it remained backward for years.

Nevis is still sugar oriented. Like St. Kitts, it is encircled by a coastal road. From practically any point on this road, a sea of cane stretches to the lower slopes of the central volcanic mountain, 3,232-foot Nevis Peak. Columbus noticed the constant cloud formations enveloping it, and so called the island "Nuestra Señora de las Nieves," "Our Lady of the Snows." (The legend, depicted in a well-known Lisbon painting by Jorge Afonso, is that a pious Roman couple prayed for divine guidance in locating a site for the church they wanted to found. While sleeping, the couple beheld an angel who told them the place would be revealed where snow fell. On the following day, a warm August fifth, flurries miraculously whit-

Chronology

Circa 1000 B.C. Indian tribes spread throughout the islands, first Ciboney, then Arawak and Caribs.

1492 Christopher Columbus discovers the New World; visits San Salvador, Cuba, and Hispaniola.

1493 Papal Bulls of Pope Alexander VI divide New World between Portugal and Spain, with Spain receiving Caribbean islands. Columbus begins second voyage; explores the Leeward Islands, Virgin Islands, Puerto Rico, Hispaniola, and Jamaica.

1498 Columbus begins third voyage; discovers Trinidad.

1502 The fourth and final voyage of Columbus; he discovers Windward Islands and Central America.

1506 First sugar mill built on Hispaniola. France challenges Spain's exclusive right to the islands by raids on shipping.

1510 Slave trade initiated to satisfy growing labor needs.

1532 Spain begins colonization of Trinidad.

1562 John Hawkins breaks Portugal's slave monopoly by purchasing African slaves in Guinea and selling them in the Spanish New World. The age of the privateer begins.

1572 Sir Francis Drake, English privateer, harasses Spanish merchant ships.

1588 Hawkins and Drake lead England to victory over the Spanish Aramada; other European countries arrive in the Caribbean.

1595 Sir Walter Raleigh visits Trinidad's Pitch Lake, and captures the Spanish governor.

1609 British party attempts to settle Grenada.

1623 England's first colony begun on St. Kitts.

1625 French, Dutch, and English settlers arrive on St. Croix.

1627 English settle Barbados.

1628 British Virgin Islands claimed by England.

1631 The Netherlands begins Caribbean colonization; eventually occupies Saba, St. Eustatius, and St. Martin, as well as Aruba, Bonaire, and Curaçao.

1632 Antigua settled by British.

1635 France colonizes Martinique and Guadeloupe.

1638 Spanish attack Hispaniola. Age of buccaneers begins.

1639 British land on St. Lucia, only to be run off in 18 months by Caribs. Parliament settled on Barbados.

1640 Barbados begins manufacture of sugar and makes rum.

1648 French and Dutch agree to a binational St. Maarten-St. Martin.

1650 Grenada receives permanent French colonists.

1652 French arrive on St. Lucia.

1655 St. Thomas occupied by Danes.

1680s Age of piracy begins.

1688 British settle Nevis.

1704 English Harbour begun on Antigua.

1717 Danes settle St. John.

1719 Daniel Defoe writes *Robinson Crusoe*.

1733 Slave uprising on St. John wrecks economy. Danes buy St. Croix from French.

1748 Treaty of Aix-la-Chapelle declares St. Lucia and St. Vincent neutral islands.

1755 Denmark declares St. Thomas and St. John free ports, open to all nations.

1756 Europe's Seven Years' War begins.

1763 Treaty of Paris allows France to retain her Caribbean islands.

1776 American ship trading in St. Eustatius receives first flag salute by a foreign power.

1781 Admiral Rodney sacks St. Eustatius.

1782 French win land battle against Brimstone Hill fortification on St. Kitts. Battle of the Saintes establishes Britain's sea supremacy in the West Indies.

1783 Spain opens Trinidad to Roman Catholic settlers.

1784 Lord Nelson arrives on station at English Harbour.

1789 French Revolution begins.

1793 Captain Bligh brings breadfruit to St. Vincent.

1794 Victor Hugues brings French Revolution to Guadeloupe.

1797 British obtain Trinidad in Napoleonic Wars.

1803 Danes end slave trading on St. Croix.

1807 Slave trading ended in English islands.

1814 England gains Tobago.

1815 Slave trading ended in French islands. Treaty of Vienna gives Virgin Islands to Danes; Curaçao, Aruba, Saba, and St. Eustatius to Dutch; Martinique and Guadeloupe to French; Grenada, St. Vincent, St. Lucia, and Dominica to English.

1820 Slave trading ended in Spanish islands.

1833 Slavery abolished in English islands.

1845 Indentured East Indian workers brought to Trinidad.

1848 Danes free slaves on St. Croix.

1856 Oil drilling begins in Trinidad.

1877 France resumes administration of St. Barts.

1902 Mont Pelée erupts, destroying St. Pierre, Martinique; La Soufrière erupts on St. Vincent, killing 2,000 people.

1917 U.S. purchases Virgin Islands from Denmark.

1945 First steel drum band appears in Trinidad.

1946 Martinique and Guadeloupe become departments of France.

1954 Netherlands Antilles formalize voluntary agreement creating a new legal basis for association with the Kingdom of the Netherlands.

1956 Establishment of Virgin Islands National Park on St. John.

1958 New tax laws bring industry to St. Croix.

1962 Trinidad and Tobago obtain independence together as a joint country.

1966 Barbados becomes independent nation.

1967 Remaining British islands in Windwards and Leewards become members of the Associated States of the West Indies.

ened the Esquiline; and there the couple built Santa Maria Maggiore, now the second oldest church in Rome.) The Spanish *Nieves* became *Nevis* when the English took over the island. Since low-cost slave labor is no longer available, Britain must provide a sugar subsidy to bolster the one-cash-crop economy. The last mill ceased operation in the 1930s, and the cane is now transported to St. Kitts for processing.

From its earliest history, Nevis profited from a unique natural attraction—thermal springs. The waters were first used as a spa by Captain John Smith's crew in 1607 while they were on their way to Virginia and the legendary meeting with Pocohontas. After some of the sailors brushed against manchineel trees (whose leaves and bark can blister the skin), the men "found a great poole, wherein bathing themselves they found much case." Five hot streams were discovered with steady flows from the island's volcano. The fame of the healing waters grew until the colonial era, when Nevis was considered to offer the most fashionable cure outside Europe. The elegant Bath Hotel, built of hand-fitted stones in 1739 at a cost of well over $100,000, is to be restored for use by jet-age travelers.

St. Christopher, which everyone calls "St. Kitts," was the first English settlement in the Caribbees. In 1623, following the arrival of Captain Thomas Warner with 13 settlers, a French warship landed with 35 men. The Frenchmen were welcomed by the British, since they offered additional protection against their common enemies, the Spanish and the Caribs. The island was divided in 1627 during a brief attempt at Anglo-French cooperation, but disrupting the noble plan two years later, the Spanish attacked, burning homes and crops and banishing settlers. Some of the displaced colonists made their way north to Tortuga, off the coast of Hispaniola, and became the original buccaneers. Others returned from their exile and continued to share St. Kitts. In 1713 the stronger British majority finally forced the dwindling French colony off the island. England maintained its control until 1782, when an incredible battle began for control of a phenomenal fortress, Brimstone Hill.

Rightfully called the "Gibraltar of the West Indies," Brimstone Hill lies on the leeward coast of St. Kitts, just northwest of the capital city of Basseterre. Rising from the sea to a height of 750 feet is the steep-walled outcropping which islanders claim to be the tip of St. Kitts's central volcano thrown over in a gigantic blast. The British decided it was an ideal site for a fort. Construction was still underway in 1782 when the Spanish conspired with the French to overpower it.

A French force of 6,000 men, supported by a substantial fleet, landed to begin the siege. When they arrived at the foot of the hill, eight English cannons and two mortars, complete with ammunition, awaited them—unarmed. The town merchants, upset with colonial authorities for allowing Admiral Rodney to sack the trading post on neighboring St. Eustatius the year before, had refused to haul the war material up Brimstone Hill. While the fight was still raging, Admiral Hood rounded Nevis Point with 22 British warships. The ensuing 30-hour sea battle marked Hood's use of a brilliant new fighting technique. Refusing to sail his ships in the courtly parade of death that traditionally pitted fleets in passing and repassing lines, Hood formed a triangle, placing anchor lines at each end of his ships. This allowed him to swing the vessels as the French sailed past, giving him two cannon shots for the enemy's one. Hood was victorious, and the French ships withdrew in defeat.

The British garrison on Brimstone Hill gained little from their compatriots' victory at sea. Each day the return fire from the fort weakened as the relentless French land forces bombarded it with their own and the captured cannons. After almost a month of struggle, the governor decided to surrender, unaware that Rodney was on his way with reinforcements. Fewer than half the surviving troops were duty-ready. The victorious French, impressed with the bravery of their adversary, magnanimously allowed the survivors to march down Brimstone Hill with full honors, carrying their arms and colors.

Much of the original fortress stonework still stands, with sev-

As trade developed between England and her Caribbean colonies, a special West India dock was built near London's Thames. Great sailing fleets lined the busy quays, unloading sugar and spice, on-loading merchandise needed to supply the remote islands.

eral ramparts unblemished. Taxis now wind up the steep road, curving past brilliant poincianas (named for a former St. Kitts governor), to provide visitors with an incomparable Caribbean view. Towering arches of hand-cut stone outline the buildings and walkways of this massive architectural feat. The top of the parapet presents an almost vertical view of the sea below and of St. Eustatius and Saba to the north. The size and condition of the stonework are testament to a monumental engineering accomplishment. There were quarters for officers and men, a hospital, ordnance stores, a kitchen, and a sophisticated drainage system which diverted rainwater into huge cisterns. When St. Kitts returned to the British after a single year of French rule, construction resumed. The fort on Brimstone Hill was completed, but never again was it challenged in battle.

As on Nevis, the sugarcane fields on St. Kitts flow almost unbroken from the coast up the steep slopes of the central volcano, 4,314-foot Mt. Misery. Ocean breezes part the sugar stalks in rippling patterns, revealing segments of a 36-mile narrow-gauge railroad. Great open-sided cars pulled by a tiny engine transport the cane to a central factory.

South of Basseterre a British firm has begun the development of an 850-acre site. Planned as a new city with complete recreational and living facilities, it is an ambitious project designed to aid the island's transition from a one-crop economy.

History, geography, and topography have played many different roles in the annals of each of these islands. The very terrain which makes Dominica unique kept it from being heavily colonized and now prevents it from being thoroughly developed. Antigua grew up around sugar commerce and a well-placed harbor; now it bases a large part of its economy on an international jet airport, duty-free shopping, industrialization, and the yacht docks at restored English Harbour. Montserrat, always a small, quiet island, remains so. Nevis lost prosperity and fame with the decline of sugar; as vacationers come in increasing numbers, it is regaining some of the stature it once had. St. Kitts's fortune fluctuated with the price of sugar, and only now is it throwing off the oppressive mantle of a one-crop economy. All the islands are seeking to reshape their futures in the light of the new and potentially most important industry of all—tourism.

Rollers "all the way from Africa" pound Dominica's wild Atlantic coast, smashing against the rocky perimeter and spraying the wind-flattened vegetation along the rugged shore. Finding no anchorage here, Columbus was compelled to sail on without landing. Dominica remains the "different" island. Nature, not man, dominates the landscape of dense woods, lush rain forests, and near vertical mountains.

Caribs live quietly on Dominica, in peaceful contrast to their cannibalistic beginnings and the raging environment about their Windward coast preserve. Handicrafts occupy the time once spent making weapons; baskets are woven so skillfully that they are watertight. Sailing prowess is a tradition. Carib ancestors made their way between islands in dugout canoes carved from giant trees. Above Castle Bruce, a native hacks away at a pole-straight gommier, transforming it into a fishing canoe. Hot rocks inside and a fire beneath the log make it pliable so that it can be spread to the desired shape. The Spaniards were so impressed with the strength and versatility of these craft that they adopted the Indian word *canoe*. A new road through the Carib reservation has opened their world to both tourism and commerce. The Indians are becoming banana growers and otherwise increasing their participation in Dominica's economy.

Nature's unspoiled glory is constantly evident on Dominica. Clouds rise over its mountainous mass and condense, replenishing divergent rivers and transforming the landscape into a primeval tropical garden.

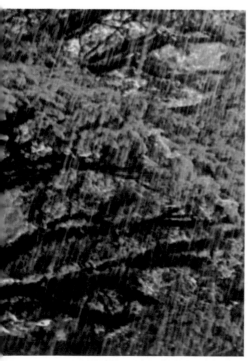

Exotic and colorful creatures are included among Dominica's diverse wild-life. Along the cool mountain streams freshwater crabs defiantly defend their territories with claws capable of inflicting serious pinches. Nearby, a two-pound *crapaud* croaks his forest refrain. The giant frog is an island delicacy, served in the hotels as "mountain chicken." High in the rain forest an *Amazona arausiaca,* one of Dominica's two parrot species, seeks protection from human predators. The birds face extinction, as they are relentlessly hunted for food.

Whether it be in the lonely quarters of the last son of a once-great planter family or in the goat-browsed forecourt of abandoned Eden Brown estate, haunting memories abound on the Isle of Nevis. Bertie Cronie has now joined his ancestors. But when he lived, those who shared his gracious company heard lively tales of the time Nevis was Europe's favorite spa. Fast ships brought London's society for a warm winter retreat and thermal cure at the Bath Hotel. Cargo holds that bore sugar to the teacups of England carried English porcelain, silver, and finery to the wealthy sugar planters on the backhaul. The day one such Nevis aristocrat was to have proudly escorted his daughter to her bridal altar, her bridegroom and his best man dueled—and died. Lavishly appointed Eden Brown, their wedding present house, never witnessed the gaiety for which it was built.

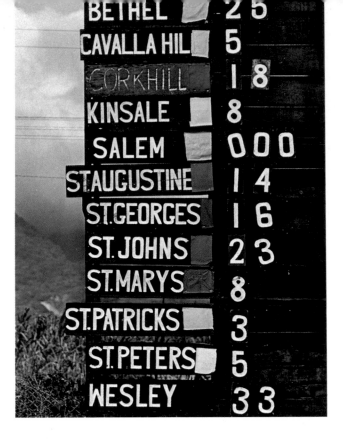

BETHEL	2 5
CAVALLA HILL	5
CORKHILL	1 8
KINSALE	8
SALEM	0 0 0
ST.AUGUSTINE	1 4
ST.GEORGES	1 6
ST.JOHNS	2 3
ST.MARYS	8
ST.PATRICKS	8 3
ST.PETERS	5
WESLEY	3 3

Montserrat, named formally by Columbus for a Spanish monastery near Barcelona, bears a nickname—Emerald Isle—that hints at a more enduring heritage. With a shamrock atop Government House and parishes like St. Patrick's to recall the Auld Sod, this verdant crown colony enjoys a Gaelic flavor bestowed by Irish colonists who arrived with Sir Thomas Warner in 1632. On the playing fields at Plymouth, contestants in an all-island track meet spring from the starting line. Even non-championship back-lot cricket displays the West Indian's verve for sports. Tourism and vacation-home building have brought many U.S. and Canadian citizens onto the island; nevertheless, lack of local job opportunities sends islanders to England for work.

Warfare is filled with ironies. The British on St. Kitts built an elaborate fort, only to see it captured during its single battle. Brimstone Hill, the "Gibraltar of the West Indies," commands a 750-foot rock outcropping by the sea. Most of the fortifications and stone quarters remain, staunchly defying time and the elements. The island's economy has always centered around sugar. When the cane ripens, cutters move through the fields with cutlasses. After the stalks are bunched, a small lift loads them onto narrow-gauge railroad cars. The track encircles St. Kitts and leads to the factory outside Basse Terre. As the world market for sugar has weakened over the years, the Caribbean Islands find production costs exceed payment. England supports prices for its former colonies.

Perfectly protected from the sea, Antigua's English Harbour housed and supplied Britain's West Indies fleet

during its glory days. Now restored, English Harbour is a favored port of call for private and charter yachts.

IV.
THE WINDWARDS

Millions of years ago great forces were at work along the curve of the Antillean archipelago. Long before the first men came, tremendous stresses gained relief by means of volcanic eruptions and land upheavals. Beginning in the Permian Period over 200 million years ago, the Windward Island chain tumultuously emerged as hot, inhospitable deserts, then sank again into the warm shallow sea for another 150 million years. Sandstone, clay, and limestone deposits settled on what had been land. About 35 million years ago, the various plates that form the earth's crust were sufficiently stressed to cause a new round of massive upheavals. In the thunderous volcanic activity which accompanied the shifting of the crust, St. Lucia, St. Vincent, Grenada, and the Grenadines were born.

Controversy raged more strongly in this small area than in any other comparable Caribbean arena. The Caribs were well entrenched by the time the first Europeans attempted colonization here. Columbus basically overlooked the Windwards, concentrating his efforts on islands to the north and south. France and England, finally taking notice, engaged in a three-way struggle with the Caribs that thwarted early development. The terrain was also a limiting factor—these were not little islands with rolling hills to clear for cane fields. They were grueling, heavily forested, rugged mountainous lands which have sections still unexplored today. History cast their lot in conflict, and in that they knew few equals.

By the 1630s, England was roaming the lower Caribbean looking for chinks in Spain's rusty armor. She had already landed settlers in St. Kitts, St. Croix, Barbados, the Virgin Islands, and Antigua. Since the Spanish were not in evidence, the British found St. Lucia (LOO-sha) was a plump prize for the taking. A Captain Judlee from St. Kitts persuaded about a hundred men from Bermuda to form a colonizing party in 1639. For eighteen months uneventful coexistence with the Caribs soothed the English into complacency. Then, an unrelated deceit brought disastrous repercussions to St. Lucia.

A British boat off Dominica supposedly welcomed some Indians aboard to trade, but once on deck they were grabbed to be

Dawn on the windward side of St. Vincent finds a farmer seeking fresh fish for his table with a throw net. The stream's waters flow into the Atlantic from the slopes of cloud-shrouded volcano, La Soufrière, 4,000 feet high.

sold as slaves. All but four fled over the rail. Hell knows no fury like a wronged Carib. Aroused natives from Martinique, Dominica, and St. Vincent organized war parties bent on revenge. With great determination and careful planning, they ignited the St. Lucian settlement on the windward side, and also they concocted a fiery precedent for modern chemical warfare by throwing red peppers into the flames. Most of the British were killed as they ran from the choking fumes.

The great misery of the St. Lucian colonists did not escape the French on nearby Martinique. France had made a rather grand presumption that all unoccupied land in the West Indies was hers. In 1642 Louis XIII attempted to breathe new life into the old *Compagnie Française des Îles des Amériques* by granting it all the Caribbean islands the Crown had illegally claimed. In addition, he made an attractive offer of nobility to anyone who would place fifty men on any island for two years. Since there were no takers and the company was still doing poorly in 1651, Louis XIV sold it to the shareholders. Governor du Parquet of Martinique, with an eye for investment, personally bought all of St. Lucia and Martinique as well as most of Grenada. But once again the Europeans had neglected to consult the Caribs. Of the first five governors du Parquet sent over, three were murdered by the Indians. It was enough to make a buyer re-evaluate his French contracts.

Claiming St. Lucia by right of prior settlement, the British were not to be outdone in plotting. "Indian" Warner, son of the founder of St. Kitts and a Carib woman, was carried to England, entertained lavishly, and presented at court. Properly primed, he was then brought back to the islands and united with 1,400 troops in warships and 600 Caribs in 17 canoes. When this imposing force landed at Choc Bay in 1664, the only question was how fast the 14-man French defense force could surrender. From then on, St. Lucia was plagued by a century and a half of Anglo-French struggle which would afford this idyllic island little peace.

During the rest of the seventeenth century the island changed hands back and forth with bellicose repetition. It was not until 1723 that anything extraordinary happened again in the "St. Lucian see-saw." As usual, both France and England massed troops, and they were particularly well provisioned. Taking a serious look at the prospects, the two commanders determined that an "effusion of blood" could be avoided by declaring the island neutral and destroying its fortifications. In an enlightened spirit, supporting affirmations came from both home governments. The French planters were elated; for such an arrangement meant no taxes, no troops to feed, and no administration to maintain. They all but dismissed the nagging problem of defense. In 1748 the Treaty of Aix-la-Chapelle further legalized the island's neutral status.

This unexpected respite lasted until 1756, when Europe's

For many years after the Caribs were eradicated from other islands, they continued to live in relative peace in the southern Caribbean. St. Vincent's neutral status allowed the Indians to become a large and vigorous tribe, but finally, European pressures were so great that the Caribs were either killed or transported from the island.

Seven Years' War brought new fighting throughout the West Indies. France fortified St. Lucia as part of her strategy, but England captured both it and Martinique six years later. The uselessness of all the battles was illustrated once again in the Treaty of Paris in 1763, which returned St. Lucia, Grenada, Martinique, and Guadeloupe to France.

One historical footnote is in some dispute. Most authorities record, as was mentioned in Chapter II, that Empress Joséphine was born in 1763 on Martinique. St. Lucians offer considerable evidence to support their claim that she was actually born on the family plantation at Morne Paix-Bouche near Castries. Her family did live on the estate until 1771, so she may have been only christened at Les Trois Îlets.

One of the charms of naval strategy in the Caribbean developed by bitter experience. Each fleet was forced to retire to other waters during late summer and early autumn to avoid the hurricane season. So it was that 1781 found the English and the French alike readying for their annual disengagement. Admiral Rodney was called back to England by Parliament to answer charges of vengefully unethical behavior in the St. Eustatius affair. De Grasse sailed northward to Virginia. His presence and assistance were invaluable in the battle at Yorktown which decided America's War of Independence.

Triumphant from his American experience, the Frenchman returned to Martinique where plans were made to unite with a Spanish force to capture Jamaica. Realizing she could not remove her best admiral, England allowed Rodney to resume his operations at Pigeon Island on St. Lucia's northwest point. Hidden below in Reduit Bay were his 36 warships and a fleet of frigates. Early in April, 1782, lookouts passed the word that the French were sailing from Martinique. Rodney set out in hot pursuit. This encounter was the decisive Battle of the Saintes, which gave England naval superiority in the Caribbean.

What the British won at war, however, they lost at the peace table: the Treaty of Versailles returned St. Lucia to France. By about 1789, autism was consuming French energies at the deadly onset of the French Revolution. Within two years even St. Lucia was flying the Tricolor and had embraced the new ideas sufficiently to be called "The Faithful." Later developments would diminish that glowing tribute. Impulsively, the new French government declared war on England. Still smarting from their recent losses in the treaty negotiations, the English attacked and captured Guadeloupe, Martinique, and St. Lucia. After a 14-hour battle, Prince Edward, father of Queen Victoria, unfurled the British flag over Morne Fortuné.

Then, in 1794, Victor Hugues brought his well-oiled guillotine to Guadeloupe. As already described, he quickly overcame the small English garrison and slaughtered the island's French planter class. Hugues was unable to capture Martinique, which spared its elite. Taking St. Lucia proved difficult, but the British finally gave in, slipping away in the night. For the next three years, Hugues used that as a base to harass the English.

The British waged yet another campaign against St. Lucia which took 18 months to succeed. By now St. Lucia had changed flags 13 times. When fighting on the Continent had dwindled and the era of battles had ended, Europe's heads of state met to straighten out their chaotic affairs. The 1815 Treaty of Vienna allotted most of the West Indies to their final owners. Guadeloupe and Martinique went to France and St. Lucia to England.

One of the interesting facets of Caribbean conquest is that islands formerly French tend to retain a Gallic flavor, whereas British occupation had little lasting effect on the culture and life of once-dominated areas. Even though St. Lucia was British-controlled from 1815 and English is the officially spoken language, place names and dialect are predominately French and the lyrical *patois* occasionally heard on some other islands is *the* language here. Blending Carib, African, and French words with local accents and rhythms creates an auditory sensation very close to singing. *Man* becomes *nom, woman* is *fam,* and *banana* changes to *fig.* *"Listen to the man"* is musically translated as *"Kuté nom-la!"* Excuse me, thank you, and *please* reveal their French derivation when spoken as *"Padoñ, mèsi, su plè."*

St. Lucia is a large island, second only to Dominica in the British Windwards. Its 28-mile length provides scenery to satisfy any taste. "Green gold," or bananas, are the new riches of the Indies, and St. Lucia leads in production. Eighty percent of its foreign exchange comes from exporting over 85,000 tons of them to England. Hill and valley are so fully planted with bananas that sunlight barely glints between the stalks. When this green tide floods out onto a wide plain, it seems to come under the moon's dominion as waves ripple across the surface and the wind sways and ruffles the leaves.

Castries, the capital, has burned so many times that little original West Indian architecture remains. After fires in 1948 destroyed three-quarters of the business district, the town was rebuilt to look more like South Florida than the Caribbean. Its virtually land-locked deep-water port is being enlarged to accommodate even more cruise ships.

Driving to the valley of Soufrière is rewarding in its diversity. The road leads over historic Morne Fortuné, then winds through

Elegant scenes from the West Indies, like this view of St. Lucia's rugged mountains, graced English drawing rooms during the eighteenth and nineteenth centuries. Such panoramas enticed many to seek their fortune in the Caribbean, where land did not have the feudal encumbrances encountered throughout the British Isles.

the lower mountains to Marigot Bay. Rapidly rising hills thatched with tropical green encompass the coconut palm fringed beach recently used as a Hollywood movie set. Marigot Harbor is sufficiently hidden from the sea so that a British fleet once eluded a French force by slipping inside and camouflaging their masts with palm fronds.

Beyond Marigot the road becomes a roller-coaster as it traverses the seaside hills. Overhanging mango trees sweeten the air and freely offer the passerby a delicious tropical feast. Sometimes a young entrepreneur will gather the mangoes at roadside and naively try to peddle them for a few cents "BeeWee" (for the old British West Indies currency). The mango is a queenly fruit. Formed like a peach, but larger, its smooth skin seems touched by Cézanne's brush—yellow, light green, blushing pink. The flavor is a golden mingling of exotic essences—tangerine, orange, coconut, pineapple, and banana: in short, ambrosia—the gods' consummate fruit.

At the end of one hairpin turn, a clearing flings apart the green veil for St. Lucia's most magnificent view, the Pitons, piercing vestiges of the island's volcanic beginnings. Gros Piton's sheer walls rise 2,619 feet from the Caribbean; Petit Piton is imperceptively lower at 2,401 feet. Their distinctive profile shapes St. Lucia into a mermaid basking in the warm sun.

A few Caribbean fishing communities retain their charm and unspoiled atmosphere. Soufrière, the quaint community below the twin peaks, is such a place. Up before dawn, the men go to sea to earn their living. Arriving at favorite grounds, they systematically play out long nets, with weights on the bottom and floats on the top, in a huge circle of chance. Patiently, the fishermen draw in the pulsating expanse to an ever decreasing circumference. Then all hands pull together to heave the flapping confusion of trapped fish on board. A full net would mean the fishing day is complete; but usually a light catch calls for another cooperative venture at a different spot. At day's end, the cream-colored nets are draped over poles to dry in the billowing wind.

Near Soufrière and slightly above it is St. Lucia's geological wonder, the "world's only drive-in volcano." A paved road actually runs between sulfurous outcroppings and steaming pools. Twenty paces from his parked car the visitor finds himself among ventings of the active caldera, a collapsed volcanic formation. Greenish-yellow coatings on rocks give the site an otherworldly cast. Strange "plop-plop-plop"-ping sounds offer surface evidence of the witches' cauldron below. Over the hill, primeval as the earth's origins, a boiling pool of black liquid rhythmically sploshes two feet above the pond as unseen pressures seek relief. The kettle-like basin reeks with corrosive smoke emanating from the bowels of our planet.

It is well documented that the underground turmoil occasionally erupting through volcanoes in specific areas is not isolated. During periods of great turbulence in the West Indies, there has been simultaneous resurgence rocking sections of Central America and northern South America. Whatever forces fuel the subterranean furnace are immense and widespread, enveloping large sections of the earth's geography. Yet, not every stress point along a recognized line of volcanic activity is affected at the same time. In 1902 the deadly eruptions on Martinique and St. Vincent occurred only one day apart and were clearly related; however, during that time St. Lucia's Soufrière, although located between the other two, changed neither in size nor intensity.

People on St. Lucia do bathe in the cooled mineral water a little downstream from its source, but there is a more secure bath site now located on Diamond Estate, a ten-minute drive from the caldera. Clear warm sulfur water flows into broad pools for out-of-doors bathing and to enclosed rooms for those desiring privacy.

These baths first gained a reputation when Baron de Laborie, the French governor of St. Lucia, collected water samples and sent them to France for analysis in 1784. Tests revealed "the same medicinal qualities as the waters of Aix-les-Bains," a popular French spa. This three-star appraisal so impressed Louis XVI that he granted funds to construct baths on the site. His Windward Island

Colonial domination manifested itself on St. Lucia in the vast officers' quarters atop Morne Fortuné. The small peak near Castries was a long-sought prize in countless battles between British and French. The old military buildings have now been converted into a new university; planned grade schools and modern facilities will turn the hill into an educational complex.

Les Canaries, a plantation on St. Lucia, as photographed 100 years ago. The long row of worker's houses, hard by the sugar mill, speaks of the slow emergence of the West Indian black from dependence — if not servitude — in an island world of limited economic opportunities.

troops enjoyed regular visits to the waters for several years after the facility was completed in 1785. During the French Revolution, the baths fell into disrepair; they have just now been reopened for public use.

On the southern end of the island at the site of a U.S. World War II airbase, a new jet airport accommodates nonstop flights from Europe and North America. From here passengers can shuttle on quarter-hour scenic flights to Castries' in-town Vigie Airport. Bordering white sand beaches, the modern hotels near town reflect the confidence of British, Canadian, American, and German investors. Along the elevated coast at the northern tip of the island, Cap Estates has begun an ambitious 2,000-acre international community to subdue the sun-seekers' wanderlust. Retirees and winter residents are buying homesites overlooking the sea. St. Lucia's first golf course and a new beach-front hotel are already open.

The north coast is as spectacular as the Maine shore or Dover. Cliffs 200 feet high plunge into driving waves, and breakers crash against the precipitous rocks. The sea seems to exhale a spray of wind-song that reaches to the very bluff-top. Wild donkeys graze here, but it is the swallows that find most delight in the magnificent solitude. Taking off from a hundred yards behind the edge, they swoop along the ground inches above the grass. Suddenly captured by the blustery updraft at the lip, they sweep skyward—wheeling, turning, rolling, free-soaring—and end their magic voyage back to its starting point.

Just offshore lies Pigeon Island, historically significant as Rodney's lookout before the Battle of the Saintes. Now, the government has just completed a sandy causeway from this future resort center to the mainland at a reported cost of over a million pounds. Hotels, a marina, and other facilities are projected along the new landfill. South of the causeway substantial activity is underway around Rodney's old anchorage. Reduit Bay boasts two fancy hotels and a club. Inland, the swampy flats have been filled with ocean-bottom sand for a proposed home and shopping complex.

Maintaining a contemporary tourist area has presented problems to most of the islands. Massive infusions of foreign capital often result in threats to local identity, land-use control, and self-government. A study assisted St. Lucians in deciding their goals lay with agriculture and tourism. Now investors know exactly what land is available for hotels, shops, and homes. Since overpopulation also poses a threat to all the islands, a family planning unit is already on the job in downtown Castries with signs that say, "You space your bananas; why not space your children?"

St. Vincent lies south of St. Lucia, close enough that misfortunes have been shared. There is some question whether Columbus ever saw the island, although he is often credited with its discovery of St. Vincent's Day, 1498. Apparently the natives powerfully discouraged any European colonization, and soon Indians from other Caribbees sought refuge on St. Vincent. With so determined a foe, the French and English decided in 1660 to call the island neutral. Unquestionably, this arrangement pleased the Caribs, but it did not long discourage the flow of European settlers. Rumors of rich soils and crops continued to attract continentals to the undefended island. Even though the Indians acknowledged a certain amount of allegiance to Charles II in 1668, tensions remained high between planters and natives. Pitched battles were common throughout the following century.

St. Vincent became a center for runaway slaves. Downwind from Barbados, it was an easy sail for Africans in makeshift boats. The island was not intensively cultivated and no great plantations existed. At first the Caribs welcomed the blacks as part of their nation; but, as Labat reported, the Africans soon outnumbered the Indians, took their women, and even started treating them poorly. Actually, the natives came to fear servitude under the former slaves whom they had befriended, and repeatedly they asked the settlers to send the Africans off the island.

The 1748 Treaty of Aix-la-Chapelle reiterated the English-French resolve relative to St. Vincent's neutrality. But soon again open warfare erupted between settlers and Indians. Only the use of

British battle troops overcame them. Survivors were banished to the undeveloped northeast corner of the island in a tract known today as "Carib Country." On the slopes of La Soufrière, they were forced to pledge a new allegiance to the English monarch.

A period of cooperation which ensued is best characterized by an incident involving the two opposing leaders. Sir William Young, then governor of St. Vincent, had just returned from leave in England when he met the Carib chief. Young had with him a white charger which he had brought from home. The chief greatly admired the animal and Young impulsively said, "The horse is yours." The Indian mounted it on the spot and rode away. At that time the government was administered from Calliaqua, on St. Vincent's southern coast. One day when the chief was visiting government house, he found Young on his veranda, gazing with pleasure at a nearby island. "You like that island?" asked the Indian. "Then it shall be yours!"—and to this day it is called Young Island.

By 1795 Carib tensions had once again exploded in revolt. Cane fields were set ablaze, and planters were afraid to leave Kingstown. Order was not restored until 1796 when Sir Ralph Abercrombie, commander of the British forces in the Caribbean, led a battle that defeated the Caribs and killed Chief Chatoyer.

Additional uprisings caused the British to round up most of the Caribs and deport them to Honduras. What was meant as punishment became a life-saving action. Ironically, the Indians left on the slopes of La Soufrière were virtually decimated in the terrible eruption of 1812. In 1902, one day before Mont Pelée's rampage on Martinique, the few struggling survivors were struck down as La Soufrière again violently exploded. It is said that only one family of "pure" Caribs remained into the 1920s on St. Vincent.

Kingstown is the essence of the old West Indies. A stroll along arch-covered sidewalks is a step back in time. Cobblestones etched by years of foot traffic surround the stone buildings. Long before air-conditioning, large porches and open windows adapted European architecture to the climate. The wooden benches and large unpartitioned rooms still used in Wesley Hall School could be from nineteenth-century tintypes.

Supermarkets and convenience stores have not replaced Kingstown's Saturday market day. Decked out in straw hats and berets, Vincentian women squat in the central square with their goods outspread before them on rough cloths. And what an array there is! A profusion of exotic aromas and sunny colors tantalizes the shopper—bananas, tomatoes, oranges, cassava, mangoes, arrowroot, coconut, cucumbers, spices, and pineapples.

When Columbus first saw pineapples, he thought them special and tried to send some back to Spain. A report described them as "scaly, like a pine cone in appearance but of a prettier shape, but soft like a melon, surpassing every garden fruit and flavor, for it is no tree but a weed, resembling the thistle or acanthus." Unfortunately, no one else knew the experience because the only sample to arrive was forthwith dispatched by the king.

St. Vincent is a planters' island, but the mountainous terrain, poor road surfaces, and thorny Carib problems precluded sugar cultivation. The money crops were those that could be grown in small clearings, such as coconuts for copra and sea island cotton. The production of the edible starch arrowroot reached over 50,000 barrels a year, before 1960. After American manufacturers found substitutes for arrowroot, the island's agriculture shifted to the new "green gold" economy.

The Mesopotamia Valley on the southeastern mountain slopes is well named, for the soil is very fertile. Even the fences are alive, formed by gliricidia cuttings poked into the ground. Terraced garden plots hang dizzily onto inclines which seem impossible to negotiate, much less harvest. On lower ridges rows of coconut palms march to the sea in geometric formation; patchwork patterns of ginger, dasheen, yams, peppers, and mangoes cling to the upper heights. Spotted throughout the valley are sustaining breadfruit trees, generous and shapely, with intricately scrolled dark green leaves.

Almost every West Indian home has at least one breadfruit

Bound for the West Indies with a cargo of Tahitian breadfruit plants, the crew of H.M.S. Bounty mutinied against the oppressive Captain William Bligh. Casting their commander adrift and his botanical specimens overboard, they returned to Tahiti for women and provisions and secreted themselves on uncharted Pitcairn Island. Bligh, surviving an epic 4,000-mile, open-boat voyage from the South Seas to Timor, returned to England. There he assumed a new command and eventually fulfilled his original mission—the transport of breadfruit plants to the Caribbean. This starchy fruit was to be food for plantation slaves.

tree. The round fruits are about the size of softballs, light green with small knobs pebbling the rough surface. A white pulpy interior gives the fruit its name and supplies a staple carbohydrate diet. Usually baked by the islanders, breadfruit is often prepared as a soup in hotels.

Captain William Bligh was sent to the South Seas to gather young plants, which, when set out in the West Indies, were to provide a cheap food source for the estate slaves. The *Bounty* crew mutinied on the Pacific voyage and Bligh, with 18 other men, was abandoned in a small boat. After three months the desperate castaways finally reached Timor Island 3,600 miles away. Later, Bligh commanded the H.M.S. *Providence* on a second journey and successfully brought 544 young Tahitian breadfruit plants back to Kingtown on January 23, 1793. From this introduction the trees now thrive on most West Indian islands, and the captain is immortalized as "Breadfruit Bligh."

A third-generation descendant, or shoot, from one of those original trees now grows in Kingstown's Botanic Gardens, the first such continued collection in the Western Hemisphere. Twenty manicured acres, reminiscent of Kew Gardens in London, have tastefully exhibited a fine selection of West Indian flora since 1765. Luckily, the rare Soufrière tree was already flourishing in the Gardens when St. Vincent's volcano erupted in 1812. Indigenous only to the slopes of La Soufrière, a precarious environment at best, the trees there were all destroyed.

It is generally thought that all the Caribbees are covered by plantations and hotels and have tourists climbing over every rock. This is certainly not the case if an island has no jetport. St. Vincent's windward coast, for example, is a series of sea-swept black sand beaches which know few visitors. The paved road ends at Georgetown on the upper east coast, leaving the northern third of the island completely unexplored by outsiders. A few estate employees on copra plantations and some mixed Caribs call these mountain slopes home. One of life's most adventurous vacations might be had exploring nothern St. Vincent in a self-drive jeep.

Within sight of St. Vincent's southern tip the Grenadines begin. They are considered by many to offer the best sailing in the world. Over 700 islands and rocks pierce the aquamarine water in the 65 miles between St. Vincent and Grenada. Few are inhabited at all and fewer still have real communities—the unparalleled prospect of vacationing among these islands is sufficient lure to attract a handsome assemblage of the world's yachts each winter. The Grenadines offer thousands of bright little beaches, complete privacy, and never-ending mountain scenery greening on the horizon.

Close enough to St. Vincent to encourage several interisland sailing races each year, Bequia (pronounced BECK-wee) is far enough away to maintain its own life-rhythm. Generations of Bequia men have constructed their sturdy ships at seaside. Rough planks are knowledgeably curved into bows that will easily part the resisting waves. Alerted by the pungent odor of boiling pitch vats, the wanderer comes upon a knot of seasoned old men making sails. Using leather palms and linen threads, they skillfully fashion the canvas in the traditional way.

Bequia is a whaling island. It is one of the last communities to send men forth in small boats to battle the world's largest mammal by hand. Every February lookouts high on the hills begin their watch for the giants that pass offshore in migration. Four boats with six men each head out to chase favorable sightings. Poised on one knee in the bow, a harpooner braces himself ready to strike. Unfortunately for the islanders, the worldwide killing of whales by large commercial operations has severely affected Bequian success. Whole seasons have passed without a single catch.

The little island did make a contribution to West Indian ethnology. When a slave ship went aground nearby in 1675, Bequia was inhabited almost exclusively by Caribs, uncharacteristically friendly to the unfortunate arrivals. The Africans were given Indian wives; their descendants were a new native combination. "Black Caribs" soon populated St. Vincent, where they ultimately outnumbered the original Caribs.

A little farther south, Mustique (pronounced Mus-TEEK) is enjoying the beginning of modest prosperity. Its asphalt runway has daily LIAT Airlines service to both Grenada and St. Vincent, and British interests have financed a housing development for retirees and tourists.

One of the problems for travelers in the Grenadines is that very few airstrips exist. Although this seclusion is eagerly sought by many vacationing sailors, it does limit the access to a remarkably attractive section of the Caribbean. On tiny Palm Island (formerly called Prune Island) a novel approach was taken. Construction of a runway came first, and then resort facilities were added. Fronting on two sides of an isolated beach, its only hotel offers comfort in a setting as remote as any to be found.

Water sports are the prime recreation on Palm Island. Day-sailors with a crew, or a Sunfish without, can be chartered. There are fishing boats with gear available to those who hope for a big catch or just a pan-fried supper back at the hotel. The waters of the Grenadines abound with a great variety—bone fish, bonito, dolphin, Spanish and king mackerel, snapper, grouper, tarpon, and yellowfin tuna for a start. Tanks, regulators, masks, flippers, weights, and a rental boat enables the enthusiast to explore nearby reefs during a brilliant morning's swim.

Of all nature's creations, none is more varied or intricate than the coral reef. Building within strict limitations, the corals are found only off the eastern coasts of the earth's continents, usually

Chatoyer, a Carib chief, led a revolt in 1795 that held the colonists on St. Vincent in terror until British troops restored order the following year.

near offshore tropical islands, within 200 feet of the surface in water above 68°F., and seldom more than 22° north or south of the Equator. Some of the liveliest polychromatic examples are found in the Caribbean.

Reefs begin when free-swimming coral larvae attach to solid supports, grow to be polyps, and begin secreting limey exterior skeletons. As their descendants multiply, the community skeleton grows, assuming a design and shape specific to that particular coral species. Billions of coral dots deposit their skeletal remains to form the familiar staghorn and brain coral sculptures. It is one of nature's incredible secrets that the lowly and insignificantly small polyp can consistently unite with its own kind to build a huge, precisely designed form.

One of the paradoxes of the reef is that very few of its living inhabitants are plants. Although they appear to grow in a spectacular undersea garden, the corals, sea fans, gorgonians, and the myriad sparkling gemlike fish are all members of the animal kingdom. Thus, fauna dominates reef ecology in the way flora prevails in heavy growth land areas.

Petit Martinique, rightfully or wrongfully, enjoys the reputation of being the smuggling center of the Grenadines. Island schooners moving northward, no matter what their destination, are always pointed out as heading for St. Barts to load up with liquor. There is also the popular story (impossible to prove) about the strict customs official from Grenada who arrived to make a thorough inspection, only to find the local residents standing somberly around a fresh grave. "Who died?" he inquired. "Nobody," came the reply. "We dug it for you."

Even with an operating airstrip and the moderately thriving village of Hillsborough, Carriacou (pronounced Carry-ah-COO) is mainly visited only by Grenadians. Formerly a sugar producer, this largest island of the Grenadines now exports limes. Its 10,000 inhabitants enjoy one of the clearest skies in the world, with stars and planets flung out in stark relief against the black void of night.

In 1609 a small group of London merchants settled Grenada (pronounced Gra-NAY-da), but constant harassment with poisoned arrows prompted them to depart within eight months. There is no doubt that the Caribs were determined to keep all invaders from their land. The next serious endeavor to colonize came in 1650, when Governor du Parquet arrived with 200 men. Although he already "owned" the island, he deemed it prudent to also purchase it from the resident Caribs with knives, hatchets, glass beads, and two bottles of brandy for the chief. Hostility soon mounted as the Indians realized they had made a bad bargain. At Sauteurs the colonists plus 300 reinforcements surrounded the Caribs on a cliff above the northern coast. As the fighting intensified, the natives recognized their hopeless position. In a last act of defiance, they threw their women and children onto the rocks below, then leapt to their own death. St. Patrick's Roman Catholic Church stands on the site of the tragic "Carib's Leap."

The worn historical pattern of ownership fluctuating between France and England was repeated on Grenada. Only after 1783 did England gain stable control.

St. George's has the most picturesque harbor in the Caribbean. Actually the crater mouth of a partially submerged volcano, the Carenage supplies Grenada with a deep-water port almost completely protected from ocean swells. Subterranean activity in 1867 caused a sudden five-foot drop in the water level of the harbor. In front of the Yacht Club the boiling lagoon expelled sulfurous vapors. Then the water rose rapidly to a height of four feet above normal. During that day the sea continued to churn up and down, causing considerable damage to anchored boats and buildings but no loss of life. Soon the Carenage waters settled to their usual tranquility, and since then St. George's has become a center for cruise ships and yacht services in the southern Caribbean. Flaring up from the quay onto the natural amphitheater formed by the surrounding hills is the town. Ice-cream-colored houses on stilts peer down at deep blue waters, pearl white boats, and Grand Anse Beach, curved by a master's compass, gleaming in the distance.

As nineteenth-century sugar beet production increased, the West Indies became backwater islands in a world that no longer warred over sugar cane fields. The emancipated slaves subsisted mainly on small plots, gradually gaining literacy and professional skills. A Briton touring the Windward Isles placed this snapshot of a market place crowd in his album.

Grenada is a microcosm of all Caribbean islands, as a driving tour will happily illustrate. Point Salines at Grenada's southern end is low sparse desert pincushioned by prickly-pear cacti. Swimmers even have a choice of sand color, since black and white beaches are adjacent to each other. Steep interior ridges underlie clouds of mist and rain forest verdure. A jade green lake called Grand Étang accents the valley below. At the northern extreme of the island, there are more white coves and enchanting views of the Grenadines—all bright, clear, and beckoning.

Long famous as the "Spice Island," Grenada has an agricultural pattern differing from that of the other Caribbees. Two factors have combined to limit the size of land holdings. Almost all the planter class was exterminated during the French Revolution; however, the high fertility of the soil and intensive cultivation have made even small parcels profitable. The valleys of Grenada nourish fruits, vegetables, and exotic flavorings—pimento, chives, cinnamon, cloves, ginger, thyme, tonka, saffron, nutmeg and mace.

Sprinkled throughout the holdings, plots of nutmeg trees dangle their apricot-sized nuts by long stems. When ripe, each golden husk splits apart far enough to disclose lacy red arils entwining a glossy brown ball. Women in processing stations deftly peel off the "mace," crack the inner shell with hard little mallets, and extract the "meg" inside. After drying and grinding, the kernel becomes the delicate flavoring nutmeg. Grenada's groves create kitchen bouquets for the world.

Although the islands in the Windward group are geographically varied, they have much in common. The Spanish never colonized this southern region of the Caribbean. England, after relentless sparring with France, finally gained political control over the islands until they became independent in 1967. Nevertheless, many French cultural traditions persist. Quiet "finds" just far enough away from the mainstream, the volcano-formed Windwards entice the tourist with scenic splendor—and seclusion.

Day's-end light glints off fishermen returning mended nets to a dugout craft near St. Lucia's Soufrière. Outboard motors ease their voyage, but stiff seas and open boats still spell danger. Across the island, jumbo jets land tourists eager to share the West Indian life-style.

The same St. Lucia sun that sparkles on blue waters and tans Englishmen encourages bananas, which ultimately brighten British breakfast tables. Preventive spraying insures survival for growing fruit. Warm winter vacations are undampened by a rainy season that lasts from June to December.

For mariners sailing up the Antillean Archipelago, the soaring slopes of Les Pitons signal arrival at St.

Lucia. Nearby, Soufrière village nestles at Caribbean edge, unmindful of its neighbor's volcanic past.

St. George's Day is a festive occasion on St. Vincent, as the dragon-slaying patron of Great Britain and the Anglican Church is also the namesake of Kingstown's Cathedral. The garb worn to the celebration by the Royal Police Force Band and Girl Guides bears witness to English cultural heritage in the Windwards. Religion ranks before politics as a Vincentian concern. There are eleven established churches on the island—the Anglican's ranking first. Many maintain their own primary schools. With only 150 square miles and nearly 100,000 population, St. Vincent and its dependencies, the Grenadines, is a heavily populated state. But mountainous terrain encourages village life, affording the visitor dramatic views of lonely volcanic sand beaches and tropical forest.

Whether it be a kitchen garden plot terraced into the Belmont Valley or a seaside coconut grove on Orange Hill Estate, St. Vincent's fertile land is intensively cultivated. Vincentian agriculture has had its problems. Though introduction of the sugar beet hastened the end of cane sugar's heyday, and the advent of cornstarch diminished demand for St. Vincent's arrowroot, the island has always been noted for agricultural innovations. Shade-loving Pangola grass, newly imported from Africa, affords rich livestock fodder and double utility for copra-producing land. Happily, coconut oil enjoys resurgent use in cleansing products. It was in answer to a petition by St. Vincent planters that the British Admiralty dispatched Captain William Bligh to Tahiti for breadfruit seedlings. His first attempt frustrated by the *Bounty*'s mutinous crew, Bligh persevered. His second voyage resulted in the introduction of the starchy foodplant as a low-cost staple in the West Indian diet. Descendants of the cargo grow in St. Vincent's Botanical Gardens.

Bequia, a Grenadine island without an airport, lives in vital contact with its surrounding seas. Here the mariner's arts of schooner building, sailmaking, and whaling make a time-honored contribution to the local economy. Not a voyage into the past, but rather a lively nautical present awaits the visitor to this dependency of St. Vincent. Sailmakers plying their craft at Bequia's Admiralty Bay can be spotted by passengers arriving on the noon mail schooner from Kingstown, St. Vincent's capital. At Friendship Bay, an interisland trader is usually on the ways—being built or repaired. And the Corea family, seamen for generations, can be seen preparing for Bequia's most adventurous involvement with the sea. Using hand harpoon or harpoon gun, Bequians are among the world's last open-boat whalers. When a whale is caught—at most only two or three are gotten each year—the iron cauldrons boil night and day, rendering blubber into oil. And whalesteaks feed all.

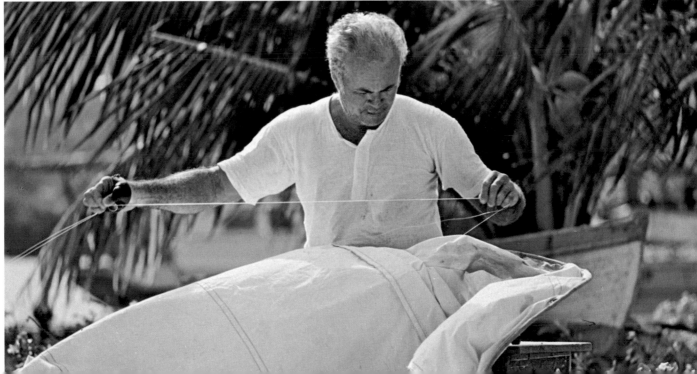

Clear, uncrowded waters make the Grenadines popular with sailors and divers. Nearby Grenada has sufficient climatic variation to support prickly pear cactus on the south coast and brilliant bougainvillea inland.

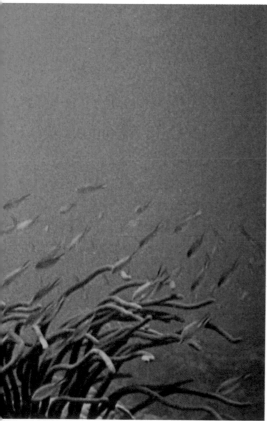

Saturday is still market day in town squares throughout the Caribbean. On Grenada, "the Spice Island," trucks and buses start arriving at dawn. By mid-morning shoppers crowd the makeshift aisles, selecting from the exotic products spread over the ground. Cacao pods dangle from trunks and limbs, like burnished ornaments on a Christmas tree. After the inside beans are dried, they are shipped abroad for processing into chocolate. A broken shell reveals both a ripe brown nutmeg and mace, the red fibrous overlay. The twin spices are processed separately and exported, along with saffron, tonka, thyme, ginger, cinnamon, and cloves.

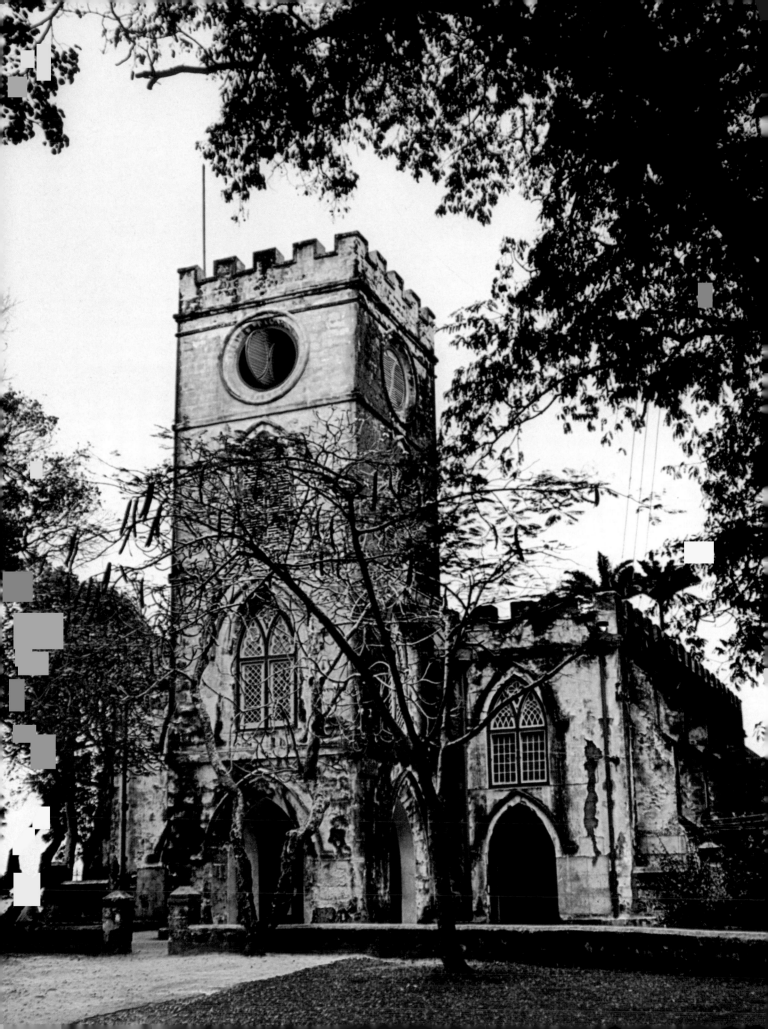

V.
THE ISLAND NATIONS

At the southern end of the Antillean archipelago two countries have sufficient resources to stand on their own in the world. Trinidad, with its companion island of Tobago, achieved independence from Britain on August 31, 1962; Barbados followed suit on November 30, 1966. Both are full members of the United Nations. Aside from this basic and very important similarity, the islands have dissimilar histories and geographic features.

Barbados, lying about 100 miles east of St. Vincent, is not a part of the volcanically formed Antilles. Built from sea deposits and coral, the limestone island was pushed upward from the ocean floor into the Caribbean sunlight during an ancient earth movement.

The unique aspect of her history is that Barbados is the only West Indies island to have known continuous rule by a single country. As a consequence, the Bajans are thoroughly British and the countryside is like an English garden transplanted to a tropical setting. The patchwork landscaping of the gently rolling hills must have been inspired by that of Kent and Devon, but here sugarcane replaces the grains and vegetables of the mother country.

Remains of shell utensils seem to establish that Arawak settlements in Barbados lasted for many years. Since the island is so far south, however, the Caribs reached it early in their northern migration, but archeological studies indicate no permanent residence.

A Portuguese sailor, Pedro a Campos, happened by in 1536 and noted in his log that the land was uninhabited. In a kind gesture he loosed some hogs to multiply and supply food for any other wanderer who might stop there. His more permanent memorial was a name. Noting that the local ficus trees had fibrous aerial roots dangling from their branches, he called the island *Los Barbados*, "The Bearded." Soon, Barbados's position of 50°30' west longitude was added to navigational maps. Honoring the Pope's dividing line (approximately 50°), Portugal made no move to claim the island; and Spain, diverted elsewhere, made no effort to settle it.

Sailing a ship owned by Sir William Courteen, Captain John Powell and his crew stopped at what is now Hopetown in 1625. Here they planted a cross and carved into a tree, "James K. of E.

Drawing heavily on English architecture, Barbados's durable churches were designed to remind the planters of their homeland ties. Eleven Anglican parishes center their religious activity within such strong coral rock walls.

and of this Island." By the end of 1628, 1,850 colonists sponsored by Courteen had established Jamestown. Overlooking the original grant, King Charles I issued "Letters Patent" for all "Caribbee Islands" to the Earl of Carlisle. Settlers loyal to this somewhat questionable courtier arrived in 1628 and established the foundation of present-day Bridgetown on Carlisle Bay. Violence between the two groups was finally resolved with remunerative payments by their patron to Courteen's benefactor, the Earl of Marlborough, and with the formation in 1639 of a representative local government, the second oldest Parliament in the British Empire. After the Carlisle Patent was surrendered to the Crown in 1663, a new agreement confirmed land titles to freeholders. Bajans fought the "hated four and a half percent," an export tax levied to compensate the Carlisle interests, until its repeal in 1838.

By 1640 Barbados had a population of 30,000 people, mainly engaged in raising sugar and tobacco. Before long, severe competition from the North American tobacco-growing colonies pushed the island into concentrating only on sugar, for which its land was eminently suited. In 1657 sugar profits were running $75 an acre (the buying power of a dollar greatly surpassed that of today's dollars), and a typical 500-acre estate could net $37,000 a year. Many landowners became wealthy even though sugar was valued at only one cent a pound. The cost of goods at the time was extremely low, shoes selling for 16¢, a pound of linen for 6¢, and a pound of thread for 40¢. "Rich as a West Indian" was an accurate expression.

Barbados began as an island of Englishmen who farmed their own plots to support their families. In 1645 there were 11,200 landholders and 5,680 Negroes. The manufacture of sugar required a factory; however, not every landowner could afford one nor could he grow enough cane to compete with the large estates. Small farmers were rapidly dislodged. They left Barbados in search of new homes elsewhere in the Caribbean. By 1667 the remaining 745 planters had increased their ownership of African slaves to 82,023.

Although the Spanish, French, and Dutch dealt almost exclusively in African natives, the English began trading in white slaves and indentured servants. They supplemented their black work force by purchasing auctioned prisoners from the Irish Rebellion, and British and Scottish soldiers from England's civil war between the Puritans and the Royalists. A more reliable source was developed by sentencing felons and by outright kidnapping, even of unsuspecting English children.

Prospective emigrants who were unable to pay their way to the West Indies could agree to five- or seven-year terms of indenture in exchange for passage, upkeep, and some money and land at the end of their service. As property, slaves were a lifetime investment whose health and well-being were of real concern to their owners. Servants, on the other hand, represented a limited value;

Decease.

Cr. 89

```
1831.                                                      Negroes, Horses, Cattle, Asses
Aug.  11  Fanny Deane      a Woman    ⎫
  "    "   Christian                  ⎪
  "    "   Jenny Margaret   a Girl    ⎬ Killed by the Hurricane    6  .  .  .
  "    "   Mary Margaret             ⎪
  "    "   Simon            a Boy     ⎭
  "   24   Thomas           a Man died of Wounds recd in the Hurricane
  "   11   1 Horse & 22 Cattle killed in the Hurricane & 9 Cattle died ⎫
                    of Wounds received in do                           ⎬   .  1  31  "
  "   24   Nancy            a Woman died   ⎫
Sept.  4  Mercy Ambo        a Girl    "    ⎪
  "   11   Jenny            a Boy     "    ⎬                              5  .  .  .
Nov.   3  Cupid                       "    ⎪
  "    4   Ben William      a Man     "    ⎭
          6 Cattle died this Year                .  .  6  .
Dec.  31  Remaining this day, carried down      166  5  65  2
1832.                                           177  6  102  2
```

all work possible was demanded from them, since their future problems were considered irrelevant. It was generally true that white indentured servants received much poorer treatment in food, care, and discipline than did white or even black slaves.

With their labor-supply problems solved, the Bajan planters consolidated estates and covered the island from shore to shore in cane. The first sugar had been manufactured as early as 1640 to "make some kind of drink for this hot climate." The refining of so much syrup just naturally led to the creation of a livelier beverage, and so rum was born! The first reference to the new drink came in 1651 when a visitor wrote of "rumbullion or Kill-Devil."

Attitudes toward rum were predictably varied. One sampler branded it a "hot, hellish, and terrible liquor"; while another, noting the problems of living in the sun, said: "Strong drinks are very requisite, where so much heat is; for the spirits being exhausted with so much sweating, the inner parts are left cold and faint, and shall need comforting and reviving."

A certain Admiral Vernon was called "Old Grog" in derision of his coarse grogram coat. When he began to water down the British naval ration of rum, his crew contemptuously dubbed the potion "grog." Nelson, on the other hand, "spliced the mainbrace"; that is, he served double daily portions to celebrate a victory.

In 1831 an overseer's precise hand chronicled the events that decreased the living assets of Mt. Pleasant Estate, Barbados. The column headings duly read: "Negroes, Horses, Cattle, Asses." Ledger entries for 1833 noted "Sam James—a boy, manumitted by an act of Parliament in consequence of his having been carried to England." Within a year, abolition of slavery began in the British Empire.

Traditionally, the last skimmings from the bottom of the copper sugar pot were mixed with water, allowed to ferment, and then distilled. The resulting dark, thick drink was greatly admired. Today's refreshments are not the same as those enjoyed by the Admirals, Rodney or Hood, since light rums are now in vogue. The continuous still, introduced in Barbados, makes them possible, and modern production techniques assure quality standards. After aging in oak casks, the liquor is colored and flavored to make the "essence of the islands." Over 660,000 gallons of rum worth almost three million dollars are exported annually from Barbados alone.

Simultaneous with Barbados's success in sugar was the establishment of Britain's colonies in North America. Fish, for which there was a ready market, became a cornerstone of their economy. New Englanders bought British cloth and hard goods, Madeira wine, and French brandy to exchange for codfish, mackerel, and herring, as well as molasses, sugar, and rum from the Caribbean. All this trade turned a tidy profit for energetic Yankee merchants.

Since both Barbados and New England were British colonies, they enjoyed favorable trading agreements. With a growing food surplus, the Massachusetts settlers developed Barbados as a market. Most of the island was in sugar, and so foodstuffs necessarily had to be imported. Planters feasted on Cape Cod mackerel and oysters while slaves were given the cheapest grades of herring and bass.

Although Holland wanted to compete for Bajan trade, England passed Navigation Acts which restricted commerce with her colonies to British ships carrying British navigators and three-fourths British crews. Barbados smarted from the sting of the provisions. Any curtailment of trade is a damaging blow to an island economy, especially one with an expanding sugar industry. Lacking water power to operate her sugar mills, Barbados resorted to horse-powered treadmills—and the horses came from New England. Barrels and casks were needed for the sugar, molasses, and rum—and Massachusetts and Connecticut forests provided wood. But the American colonies would not be free until 1781, and the Navigation Acts were destined to affect the remaining British colonies into the nineteenth century. Barbados could only suffer the restrictions.

The planters' life offered its compensations. Sugar was relished in Europe, and the elements cooperated to produce large crops. By 1700 there was an elegant English manor atmosphere about the island. Importing so many of the good things in life drew a diaphanous curtain of gentility before the realities of a tropical province. While visiting Barbados the ubiquitous Father Labat wrote: "One observes the wealth and good taste of the inhabitants in their furniture, which is very fine, and their silver, of which they have so large a quantity that were the island to be sacked the silver alone would be worth more than the value of several galleons."

Sugar's golden days turned dark in the early nineteenth century as the abolition movement swept the world. England had been wrenched by internal strife about slavery for decades before Parliament finally passed a ban on slave trading in 1807. Bajan planters, who depended so heavily on slave labor, stiffened for the next blow. Abolition came on August 1, 1834. Complete disorganization was supposed to have been averted by the adoption of a six-year transitional apprentice system, but the former slaves became restless and demanded removal of the legislative shackles that still restricted their lives. Total freedom was granted on Emancipation Day, August 1, 1838. For their losses the planters received 1,750,000 pounds sterling from the British government. Inevitably, many unskilled former slaves stayed on at their old plantations.

Two firm, though paradoxical, legacies of English rule have sustained the island. One is the importance of education: the most densely populated country in the Western Hemisphere also has the highest literacy rate—above 97 percent! Compulsory schooling until age 14 is based on the British system. Students who qualify can attend a local branch of the University of the West Indies.

The second legacy is the prevailing concept of law and "Parliamentary" order. An observer of a Bajan courtroom might well believe himself in a London tribunal, for the island judges still don the traditional English wigs and robes. Fortunately, a falling gavel

A turn-of-the-century postcard from Bathsheba, Barbados, is a harbinger of the tourist industry that now is so vital to Bajan life. The proudly displayed coastal scenes awaited only the jet plane to become a major attraction for winter-weary neighbors to the north.

no longer portends a desperate choice between hanging or slavery.

The economy of Barbados is a heady blend of sugar, molasses, rum, and—tourists. There is a new deep-water port that can accommodate eight large cruise ships simultaneously. Nonstop jet facilities bring a host of visitors to stay at the band of ocean-front hotels around two sides of the island. The beaches are among the finest in the Caribbean. Thriving in Barbadian tax concessions, modern air-conditioned factories produce millions of computer memory cores for export. The Barbados Development Board is actively recruiting other industries to utilize the skills and diligence of the workers with African ancestry.

In the deep waters offshore, unusually numerous schools of silvery flying fish take wing in sequence. Their aerial agility delights charter-boat tourists, and their fine flavor assures the livelihood of 2,000 Bajan fishermen. Since abolition, the island has developed its own fishing industry now netting over ten million tons annually. Sixty percent of the catch is the exotic specialty that gives Barbados the romantic title, "Land of the Flying Fish."

Bridgetown's vigorous activity revolves around the Careenage. Colorful island schooners line the wharves, unloading bananas from the Windwards and cement from Trinidad. Across the bay a large native woman ponders her pair of citrus crates with a classic shipping complaint, "But ah ordered *two* 'grapefroot' and *two* 'au-range.' " Down the way where the harbor and the Caribbean meet, an impromptu fish market attracts buyers and gawkers. "Ten flyin' fish for dollah . . dat's cheep," calls a woman squatting between several baskets brimming with tuna, snapper, and bonito as well. A nearby competitor counters with, "Ah got dolphin! It's cheep too . . and go-o-od!" Quietly protective of the harbor from his pedestal in Trafalgar Square stands Lord Nelson, elevated here a full 27 years before London so honored him.

The surface of Barbados is inclined toward the east, where all three of its underlying formations are exposed to the windward elements. Cars can be parked on coral-topped Hackleton Cliff (1,100 feet). About three hundred feet beneath the precipitous drop is sandwiched a thin section of chalklike deposits of the Oceanic Series. Huge rocks of the foundation Scotland Series are apparent along the shore, dramatically manifested in dark weathered boulders silhouetted by the sparkling beach at Bathsheba.

The little-frequented Atlantic coast looks much as it did two centuries ago, although Barbados was then more densely populated than either Holland or China. Today there are more than 1,500 Bajans per square mile, whereas humanity-packed China practically luxuriates with only 120 people per square mile. The wonderment is that, from the air, Barbados appears to be almost uninhabited. Expanses of sugarcane give the illusion of space, and shade trees conceal settlements of over a quarter million islanders squeezed into 166 square miles.

Bajans are a happy and friendly people, proud of their homeland and proud of its independence. Their feelings find expression in a popular calypso refrain offered nightly at beach-front hotels: "Ah love de people in dis countree, Barbados is mah happy home."

Located only six miles off the coast of Venezuela, Trinidad is just barely in the Caribbean; yet, as the birthplace of calypso, limbo, and the steel band, it is very much a West Indian island. When Columbus discovered Trinidad on his third voyage in 1498, it was still the home of the Arawak. These hardy natives had survived many Carib raids to remain on their island, only to be virtually eradicated by the Spanish colonists who settled here.

But the fragility of Spain's claim to the New World was made obvious once again as Sir Walter Raleigh sought to regain his lost favor at court. In his effort to stop "declining and falling into a recess," as he put it, he became consumed with the golden dream of finding *El Dorado*. Sailing along the western coast of Trinidad, Raleigh discovered what would someday be worth far more than any mythical golden city. He spotted a lake of natural asphalt. Although this was later to lead the island into the petroleum era, to him Pitch Lake only meant caulking for his ships. He described it as "most excellent good," noting that it did not melt in the sun the way the Norwegian product did and estimating there was

English claims to Trinidad began after Sir Walter Raleigh captured the old capital of San José in order to immobilize his Spanish competition. He was in the New World seeking the mythical city of El Dorado, thought to be somewhere up the Orinoco River in South America. That fabled vision of golden buildings set on golden streets had enraptured many a gullible dreamer. Raleigh returned to an England that mocked his unsuccessful quest.

enough "that all the ships of the world might be laden from them."

To avenge the many wrongs done the Indians by the Spanish and to secure an escape route, Raleigh sacked the capital of San José (now St. Joseph) and captured its Governor Berreo. Then he entered Guiana and claimed it for Queen Elizabeth. The month-long quest proved not only difficult but futile: its account was doubted by many at court.

Meanwhile, the Spaniards regained control of Trinidad. But they continued to find the island unprofitable, and by the 1780s the outlook was so bleak that the king was persuaded to allow non-Spanish immigrants. This unprecedented invitation to settle on a Spanish island attracted mainly French colonists from other Carib-bees. To be admitted, the newcomers had to profess at the dock that they were Roman Catholics. Africans lined up with rag-tag whites to swear by their adopted religion. (Prejudice was obvious, however, since free blacks got only half the land grant that whites did.) A compelling attraction was the ruling that any debtor arriving here to settle was free of all past liabilities. In the days of debtors' prisons and long jail terms for even minor offenses, this ruling alone was sufficient to fill the boats. The new Trinidadian riffraff was held in such low esteem by other nations that Grenada, for instance, required each of these particular visiting neighbors to post a thousand-pound-sterling good-behavior bond—or be considered a vagabond.

The French immigrants introduced cane cultivation but never realized any of the profits, because the French and Spanish war with Britain cost Spain Trinidad in 1797. After transforming it into a Sugar Island, the English faced complete disaster with the abolition of slavery in 1834. They solved their problem by importing British subjects from India. Beginning in 1845, as many as 3,000 indentured laborers a year started their five-year bondage periods. Immigration of these servants ended with World War I, but by then over a third of the population was of East Indian heritage. Today, Trinidad's people have a minglement of ethnic origins—Africa, India, China, Portugal, Venezuela, England, Spain, and France, among others.

In 1962 Trinidad and Tobago, as a single country, became an independent member of the British Commonwealth of Nations and the United Nations. Seated in Port of Spain, Trinidad, the constitutional government consists of Her Majesty's appointee, the Governor-General, along with the Senate and the House of Representatives. As in Barbados, real power rests in the House, just as it does in England. Trinidad and Tobago are divided into 36 constituencies, each electing one member to the House. The leader of the majority party is named Prime Minister. Senators are appointed by the Governor-General on the advice of the Prime Minister and the Leader of the Opposition. Normally, the term of office for both branches is five years. Over a million islanders are now united under the red, white, and black national colors, appropriately symbolizing the sun, the sea, and the earth.

Because it is a big continental island, Trinidad has a much larger and totally different bird population from the rest of the Lesser Antilles. Its fauna represents species found on the nearby South American mainland. There are cotingas, antbirds, oilbirds, ovenbirds, and several varieties of hummingbirds. Venerating these sparkling little acrobats, the native Arawak called their home *Iere*, or "Land of the Hummingbirds." Southeast of Port of Spain is the 10,000-acre primeval wilderness of Caroni Bird Sanctuary. Guided boat tours can be taken through the network of mangrove-lined channels to watch herons, snipes, egrets, and many kinds of ducks living here. The region is a significant breeding ground for brilliant scarlet ibises, fishing in the mud with long down-curved bills.

Even Tobago, smaller and farther away from South America, has 60 indigenous bird species and 450 acres of protected area. The whole of Little Tobago, a tiny satellite isle solely designated as a sanctuary, serves as the adopted home of the rare birds-of-paradise. They have been maintained as a "wild" attraction since their introduction from the Aru Islands of Dutch New Guinea in 1909. All these areas on Trinidad and Tobago are the natural "vacation habitats" of migrating birds from North America.

Oil is the backbone of Trinidad's economy. Drilling began near Pitch Lake in the late nineteenth century, but commercial quantities were not found until the early 1900s. Since then, oil has given the island the highest per capita income in the West Indies. One third of Trinidad's revenue and four-fifths of its exports are petroleum related. By the 1960s over 3,000 wells were producing black gold, about a fifth of them offshore in the Gulf of Paria. Although Trinidadian wells yield only .5 percent of the world's consumption, Texaco's refinery at Pointe-à-Pierre processes vast quantities of South American oil—nearly ten million gallons a day.

This singularly most valuable industry in the West Indies is fraught with difficulties. Trinidad is simultaneously blessed with oil and cursed with broken Tertiary rock formations which allow the viscous prize to collect in small pools. A good producing well in the Middle East will pump over a hundred times as much as the average Trinidadian well. Only half the island's oil surfaces by its own pressure; the remainder has to be slowly pumped. And offshore drilling is expensive—each dry hole means a loss of several million dollars. Since Trinidad's fields yield different types of crude oil, the refinery has to treat each one specially, adding time and expense to an already costly process.

The Pitch Lake Raleigh found is important in Trinidad's present-day economy. Created by seepage from an underground oil pool, the almost circular lake covers about 95 acres. Although walk-

ing leaves imprints, the pliable surface is firm enough to be safe. Workers saw the pitch into sizeable chunks during the daily mining process. These are taken to a nearby processing plant, and heat is used to force out any trapped water. Then the viscous asphalt is poured into wooden kegs, where it hardens into blocks. About half the annual 150,000-ton output is exported for road-building. Sample drilling indicates that the center depth reaches over 250 feet, but each year the surface is a few inches lower. Mining is consuming the lake, which does not appear to be replenishing itself; still, Pitch Lake is the largest source of natural asphalt in the world.

Agriculture and manufactured goods provide the remainder of Trinidad's non-tourist income. Sugar, citrus, bananas, coconut, and cocoa are all grown for trade; and rum, beer, and a host of finished items gyrate from assembly lines. Best known of the island's products are calypso records featuring Trinidadian music.

Synonymous with festive gaiety in the tropics, *carnival*, from the Latin *carne vale*, means "farewell to the flesh." And what a goodbye it is! This 200-year-old tradition bursts into life the week before Ash Wednesday. An entire year's effort has gone into the songs and costumes, designed to entertain every participant and bring still more fame to the King of Carnival. Incredibly elaborate gaudery, often costing hundreds of dollars in materials, appears to defy gravity and imagination. Woven together from wire, metal, leather, beads, flowers, and papier-mâché, fantasy figures jounce, bob, and glide along the street, supported only by the reveler beneath. On the final Monday and Tuesday of the celebration, Port of Spain is overwhelmed with that distinctive civic association, the Carnival Band. Over a hundred different groups take to the streets, each attempting to outdo all the others in costumes and song competition. The 400 to 4,000 members in each band blend sound and color until the whole island swings into a singing, pulsating frenzy. New calypsos rapidly become old favorites as the street intersections sway with communal dancers so tightly pressed together that only their heads can keep time to the catchy beat. Other islands may have carnivals, but none is bigger or more boisterous than this celebration. Trinidad has THE carnival to experience!

A Trinidadian invention gives calypso its distinctive sound. After it was first seen during a carnival in the early 1930s, the steel drum was for years only a rhythm instrument. During World War II the U.S. military discarded huge piles of used oil drums. Heat tempering was accidentally found to improve the tone. Eventually, a creative mind reasoned that segmenting the surface would provide individual notes—and a new musical instrument sounded out!

Victory celebrations in 1945 brought the first of the new "pans" onto the streets. Islanders loved their vibrant polyphony. Nearly spontaneous bands with dozens of steel drums were formed, and reverberated with calypsos, pops, classics, and even hymns. Carnival refrains, bobbling over the waves, could almost reach the final island in our golden chain—Tobago, only 21 miles away.

On the title page of the original 1719 edition of *Robinson Crusoe,* Daniel Defoe described his deserted island as located "at the mouth of the mighty Oroonoka [Orinoco] 30 miles N. of Trinidad, an island lying just in the Caribbean Archipelago." Today, various accommodations carry the name of the fictional sailor, and Tobago is known as "The Robinson Crusoe Island."

So many countries coveted Tobago that the first 80 years of the seventeenth century saw it change hands 20 times. France, Holland, Flanders, and Courland (now a part of Latvia and Lithuania) all tried repeatedly to gain control, only to see England granted title in 1814 after the Napoleonic Wars.

Early in the 1800s some 15,000 slaves succeeded in taming the entire landscape into their masters' dream. The expression "rich as a *Tobago* planter" grew out of Tobago's five decades of unsurpassed supremacy as a Sugar Island. Abolition and the fierce 1847 hurricane took their tolls, but business recovered so well that by 1870 the island was exporting almost five million pounds of sugar and 115,000 gallons of rum a year. Tobago's exclusive English broker declared bankruptcy which set off an economic decline in the island. Sugar production had deteriorated so much by 1889 that voluntary attachment to Trinidad became necessary.

In the serene, deeply forested hills, there is no indication today that for centuries Tobago was the center of deadly European conflict or that the island was ever fully planted with sugarcane. Victorious rain forests again cover the mountain slopes with tangled growth. The varied calls of cocricou, mot-mot, manakin, and wren mix with the jungle sounds of tree frogs cheeping and giant bamboo rhythmically clicking in counterpoint.

Still basically agricultural land, Tobago is opening its southern region to tourist development. Several attractive hotels front on pastel sands often shared with native fishing fleets—the dawn swimmer may find himself alongside a score of villagers hauling in a net full of grunts, kingfish, and snapper.

Unusual "walk-in" Buccoo Reef can be reached by glass-bottomed boats leaving from several points. After the anchor is set three miles offshore in the shoals, even nonswimmers can wade across the solid bed of coral to see the reef. Aided by face masks, visitors can peer through coral crannies for a nose-to-nose view of hundreds of fish swimming unpretentiously in review.

Tobago still has deserted beaches without a trace of Friday's footprints to mar their isolation. Given one image, the island dream would surely be: a remote strand curving out of sight in both directions toward a far horizon; fluctuating surf continually blowing and dissolving sea-foam castles of shimmering iridescence; crunchy sand warming bare toes; long days lazing in the sun; a free spirit communing with the wide world. Anyone contemplating such a rendezvous might well muse with the poet Robert Louis Stevenson,

> I should like to rise and go
> Where the golden apples grow;
> Where below another sky
> Parrot islands anchored lie,
> And, watched by cockatoos and goats,
> Lonely Crusoes building boats: . . .

Tobago, the last of our discovery islands, is a magic place. Though largely unknown, it is a land meant to be discovered, savored, and left unspoiled.

Adventure in the Antilles is neither beginning nor ending—it is only continuing. Shaped to the convenience of European powers, the long history encompasses both pathos and promise of settling a New World. Now the power to determine their future has come home to the residents of the West Indies. Although the 500-year fortune hunt is past, travelers can always personally discover the richly rewarding beauty of the golden islands of the Caribbean.

For over three centuries, Barbados has been creating its own happy blend of British and island cultures. A necklace of white sand beaches lures an international clientele of vacationers. They find the climate healthy and invigorating, the cuisine a marriage of tropical offerings and cosmopolitan recipes, the Bajans a delightfully resourceful people.

In Barbados, representative government under British law reaches back to 1639, making its parliament the second oldest in the Commonwealth. Traditions are strong on an island that never changed its allegiance. Since 1966, Supreme Court Justice, police guard, and policewoman all work within the framework of a newly independent country whose legal system is based on time-honored British precedents.

Independent Barbados still treasures British tradition. At Bridgetown's center, Trafalgar Square, a statue of heroic Lord Nelson was firmly in place 27 years before London duplicated the honor. Long dependent on sea trade, Barbados continues to export sugar, rum, and molasses. As a lightly industrialized nation, she must import food and finished goods. Island schooners sail into the "careenage" bringing supplies from fellow members of the Caribbean Free Trade Area, CARIFTA. Organized in 1968, CARIFTA spurred commerce immediately, increasing Barbados's exports to four member islands from 2.4 million pounds sterling in 1968 to 3.4 million pounds two years later.

Carnival explodes on Trinidad's streets with costumed revelers dancing and singing to calypso favorites.

During the week before Lent, all other activity ceases as islanders enjoy the Caribbean's biggest festival.

Fertile imaginations create wildly ornate costumes, reflecting Trinidad's African, European, and Asian heritage. Prizes for best new song, individual costume, and musical band are presented by the Carnival's King.

No island has woven as many foreign threads into a national fabric as Trinidad. People, institutions, and buildings reflect these diverse contributions. Mediterranean, Victorian, and Muslim architectural styles are all present; the population potpourri makes Trinidad the "melting pot of the Caribbean." When England captured the island from Spain, more French were found here than Spanish. This heady mixture continues with African descendants forming a majority and East Indians comprising a third of the population.

Steel drum bands and calypso music are synonyms for the "sound" that Trinidad has given the world. Before World War II, the island musicians used bamboo drums to accompany their African-inspired melodies, but the fragility of bamboo and the availability of surplus oil drums led to the happy discovery of a new instrument. By heat-tempering the drum's top and arc-cutting its length, the inventive Trinidadians transformed the hollow-thudding discard into the mellow sounding "pan." The world now associates its gentle tones with sunny island beaches. Picnickers from Port of Spain, fleeing their industrially utilized shoreline, enjoy touring the beautiful northwest coast. Catchy calypso rhythms and clever lyrics combine to create witty social commentary. No island trend or personality has "arrived" until a calypso refrain has been sung in merry disdain.

So many tourists have bypassed Tobago that she remains a natural, unspoiled garden. The frangipani caterpillar stretches its five-inch length while a red-crowned woodpecker feeds its youngster ripe bananas.

Afterword from the Author

This book is lovingly dedicated to Charlotte, whose ceaseless devotion and tireless efforts made it all possible.

Many other people and organizations made significant contributions to the project. Sincere thanks are given to the numerous friends who offered advice and support. The National Geographic Society was responsible for a series of long Caribbean assignments which provided a background for this book. Black Star, my agent, has been a stalwart support. Special thanks goes to my parents who provided a quiet place and an understanding atmosphere in which to do the writing.

Wendy Jolly and the Eastern Caribbean Tourist Association made valuable arrangements and suggestions as did Kenneth McLean of Court Line in England. BWIA, LIAT, BOAC, and Windward Island Airways aided in needed transportation assistance. In the Virgin Islands, Caneel Bay Plantation on St. John and Hallie and Mike Goulet on St. Croix's Charte House were most helpful. In the Dutch islands, Julian Conner of the St. Maarten Tourist Bureau, Frank Hassell of Saba's Tourist Board, and Lee Bauer on Statia supplied aid and information. Remy de Haenen gave assistance on St. Barts, while Roger Fortuné of Guadeloupe's Tourist Board and Jacques Guannel of the Department of Tourism of Martinique generously provided many services. Club Méditerranée was an enjoyable stop midway through the last island tour. Yvonne Maginley of the Antigua Tourist Board was very cooperative.

Very special thanks always goes to Pete and Margie Brand of Island House, whose generosity is as boundless as Dominica's delights are endless. Irwin Skeete of St. Lucia's Tourist Board and Gillian John of St. Vincent's Tourist Board were enthusiastic in showing off their islands. At the Palm Island Beach Club, the whole Caldwell family joined into helping obtain pictures, while Gertrude Protain of Grenada's Tourist Board offered information and sources regarding her favorite island. Lucille Seemungal of the Tourist Board of Trinidad and Tobago made great efforts to assure a balanced view of her islands. The Barbados Tourist Board checked the many historical facts for accuracy.

Dr. Charles Hoffman, a long-time Caribbean scholar, read the material for factual content and offered meaningful suggestions. Four libraries made the research possible and pleasant: the Library of Congress, the University of Miami Library, the University of Florida Library, and the Montgomery Co. (Md.) Public Libraries.

Ted Spiegel conceived the book and had the tenacity and faith to see it through. Lee Wilfert helped him with the design effort. Finally, Crown Publishers offered both confidence in the project and suggestions that helped strengthen the final product.

To all I give my heartfelt thanks.   F.W.

Index

Numbers in *italics* refer to illustrations.

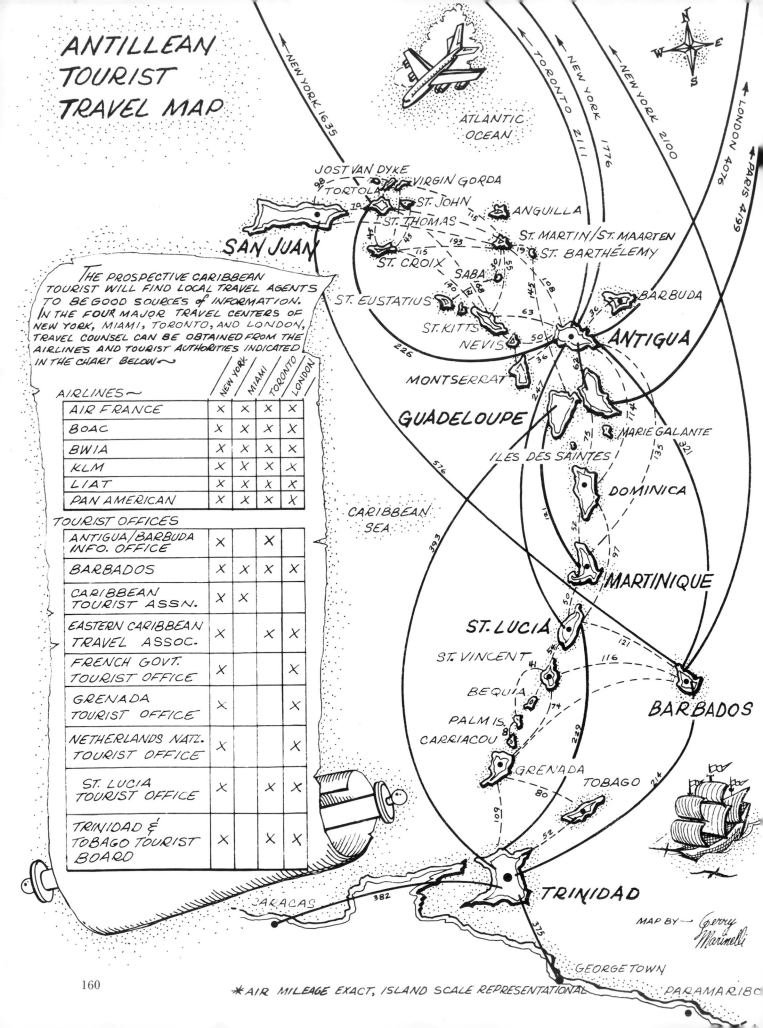

ANTILLEAN TOURIST TRAVEL MAP

THE PROSPECTIVE CARIBBEAN TOURIST WILL FIND LOCAL TRAVEL AGENTS TO BE GOOD SOURCES OF INFORMATION. IN THE FOUR MAJOR TRAVEL CENTERS OF NEW YORK, MIAMI, TORONTO, AND LONDON, TRAVEL COUNSEL CAN BE OBTAINED FROM THE AIRLINES AND TOURIST AUTHORITIES INDICATED IN THE CHART BELOW~

AIRLINES~	NEW YORK	MIAMI	TORONTO	LONDON
AIR FRANCE	X	X	X	
BOAC	X	X	X	X
BWIA	X	X	X	X
KLM	X	X	X	X
LIAT	X	X	X	X
PAN AMERICAN	X	X	X	X

TOURIST OFFICES	NEW YORK	MIAMI	TORONTO	LONDON
ANTIGUA/BARBUDA INFO. OFFICE	X		X	
BARBADOS	X	X	X	X
CARIBBEAN TOURIST ASSN.	X	X		
EASTERN CARIBBEAN TRAVEL ASSOC.	X		X	X
FRENCH GOVT. TOURIST OFFICE	X			X
GRENADA TOURIST OFFICE	X			X
NETHERLANDS NATL. TOURIST OFFICE	X			X
ST. LUCIA TOURIST OFFICE	X		X	X
TRINIDAD & TOBAGO TOURIST BOARD	X		X	X

ATLANTIC OCEAN

NEW YORK 1635
TORONTO 2111
NEW YORK 1776
NEW YORK 2100
LONDON 4076
PARIS 4199

JOST VAN DYKE
TORTOLA
VIRGIN GORDA
ST. JOHN
ST. THOMAS
SAN JUAN
ST. CROIX
ANGUILLA
ST. MARTIN/ST. MAARTEN
ST. BARTHÉLEMY
SABA
ST. EUSTATIUS
ST. KITTS
NEVIS
BARBUDA
ANTIGUA
MONTSERRAT
GUADELOUPE
MARIE GALANTE
ILES DES SAINTES
DOMINICA
CARIBBEAN SEA
MARTINIQUE
ST. LUCIA
ST. VINCENT
BEQUIA
PALM IS.
CARRIACOU
GRENADA
TOBAGO
BARBADOS
CARACAS
TRINIDAD
GEORGETOWN
PARAMARIBO

MAP BY— Gerry Marinelli

* AIR MILEAGE EXACT, ISLAND SCALE REPRESENTATIONAL